Essays

Essays
© 2023
All rights reserved.

ISBN: 979-8-9861352-0-5

Front cover and book design: Blair Johnson
Back cover design: Abbey Frederick

Essay Press is a non-profit 501(c)(3) organization dedicated to publishing innovative, explorative, and culturally relevant writing.
www.essaypress.org

Distributed by Small Press Distribution
1341 Seventh Street
Berkeley California 94710
spdbooks.org

Essays

Ariel Goldberg
Ken Chen
Wayne Koestenbaum
Tracie Morris
Anaïs Duplan
Raquel Salas Rivera
Brandon Shimoda
Cecilia Vicuña
Fred Moten

Edited by Dorothea Lasky
Afterword by Mónica de la Torre

Brick and brick and brick may make a house—that house a haptic and optic riff of brick. Pattern's a sense language.

—Douglas Kearney

CONTENTS

11   Introduction, *Dorothea Lasky*

LOGIC, AESTHETICS, MEANING, AND MEMORY IN A POEM-ESSAY

17   Just Captions, *Ariel Goldberg*
33   Antiwest or The Beginning, *Ken Chen*
43   The Cheerful Scapegoat, *Wayne Koestenbaum*

THE ESSAY, THE MANIFESTO, AND THE POETIC IMAGINATION

51   Poetry, the Body, Manifesto, *Tracie Morris*
59   A Poet's Essay is a Conversation, *Anaïs Duplan*
69   Burning Cane Fields, *Raquel Salas Rivera*

CONTRADICTIONS, THE SEA, AND THE SNOW: A POEM-ESSAY AS THE OPEN SPACE

79   Four short and unfinished essays (with poems) from the ruins of Japanese American incarceration, *Brandon Shimoda*
89   The Poet's Essay, *Cecilia Vicuña (transcript)*

99   recess and nonsense, *Fred Moten*

115   What is an Afterword, *Mónica de la Torre*
123   The Poet's Essay Q&A —Transcription

INTRODUCTION   *Dorothea Lasky*

Before we begin, I'd like to take a moment to thank the poets who have contributed to this volume. It is beyond belief that such esteemed poets and writers agreed to share their voices and perspectives, and to be part of this conversation. It was outside of my wildest dreams to have my poetic heroes be a part of this endeavor, and I can't ever thank all of them enough for their generosity.

This book was inspired by a symposium held in March, 2018, at the Columbia University Lenfest Center for the Arts, called "More Than a Manifesto: The Poet's Essay." The day of the symposium was organized into several parts. There was a series of short talks, organized loosely around three themes. The day started off with presentations from Ariel Goldberg, Ken Chen, and Wayne Koestenbaum, who wrote pieces under the theme of "Logic, Aesthetics, Meaning, and Memory in a Poem-Essay." Next, Tracie Morris, Anaïs Duplan, and Raquel Salas Rivera presented, writing under the theme, "The Essay, The Manifesto, and The Poetic Imagination." After a short break, there were presentations by Myung Mi Kim, Cecilia Vicuña, and Brandon Shimoda under the topic, "Contradictions, The Sea, and The Snow: A Poem-Essay as the Open Space." Each group of three talks was followed up by a Q&A to let some of the ideas proposed by our presenters unfold. In the evening, Fred Moten delivered his keynote address.

The inspiration behind the symposium arose in my classrooms, particularly at Columbia. In my classes, especially my undergraduate ones, I often have given the assignment to my students to write a poet's essay, so as to complete, at least in part, a requirement for the course that didn't involve actually writing poetry. I have always seen this assignment as a sort of a curricular intervention, as a way to ask them to write an essay, which is not on its face critical or academic in nature, but a poet's creation.

This task would often confuse or delight them and probably most of the time, do both. They would often ask me what this could possibly mean. *A poet's essay? Does this have to have an argument*, they would ask? My answer: always, or not necessarily. Or more often than that, my answer to their questioning: no, no, it doesn't. There would often be more questioning when I told them to not think about essays they had written before for their other classes, when they were writing this one. I am not sure I answered any of their questioning well. In many ways, I created the symposium and this book to help answer their questions about the assignment, and my own.

The ideas behind my poet's essay assignment seemed simple to me at first of course, but with their questioning soon became complex. Really I was asking them to work against the form of the essay they had gotten so used to in their other classes, and this created a kind of valuable, educative tension. Or at least I hope it did. It is true that the essay form, especially in our country, has become both a symbol and an enactment for a kind of stilted learning, a fault or limitation of the imagination, an SAT response to the question of nothingness, existence, and radical love. Bahumbug!

Because if we think of something as banal to many of us as the 5-paragraph essay, we can see how the root of a limitation in our imaginations take shape. Obviously, this overused form is something that a writer may or may not work against, but for the children living in our nation right now, this is the end goal of much of their education up until at least 12th grade, especially if they are lucky and are going to a school that hopes to prepare them for advanced learning and a career. But even in our esteemed universities, perhaps the point too is to write a 5-paragraph essay, albeit with sophistication, to take the form and do it "well." It is perhaps the idea that to have an elegant point, and to prove it well, is the point. That is as far as so many people ever get in their thinking about the matter.

This is not to suggest that argumentation is inherently wrong, or evil even. Quite the contrary, I believe the construction of a thesis as a projected outcome to set out and then to carry through is a worthwhile academic endeavor. It certainly is correct in many fields, to have a projected goal or plan. I just don't think it is the only, valuable way of creating or narrating a path of one's own thinking. And I also don't think it gives space for the aesthetic logic necessary for the creative process, which is perhaps the most holy space of all.

Poetry as both a form and genre has many possibilities to exist within; however, poetry too oftentimes has the burden to have an argument and a set of imagery and meanings that are preconceived and placed within the poem. In this way, poetry gets conflated with writing a thesis or project, and the poet simply the presenter of perfectly argued language. In addition, when poets attempt to bridge the gap between genres and write within the contemporary essay form, they are tasked to construct perfect arguments there as well and avoid the associative and aesthetic logic that makes poems important. The term *essay* itself was coined by Michel de Montaigne in the 1500s, and it comes from the French word, *essai* which means to test or experiment with what one knows as a learning tool (and is in some opposition to the terms we use to discuss the essay now, such as thesis).

As we move forward, deeper into this new century, I want our thinkers and writers to move beyond this linear thinking into the realm of what an essay by someone like Montaigne might do. His essays do as they say they will—they test out ideas, they are unafraid to get messy in their execution, they are brave enough to go forward into the uncharted waters. In them, it's completely beside the point to get back to where they started, let alone where they'd say they would go. They are simply beside the point. It's true.

In *Releasing the Imagination: Essays on Education, the Arts, and Social Change*, Maxine Greene, writing of the imagination, in many ways sums up the core of this book:

> Once again, this is where imagination enters in, as the felt possibility of looking beyond the boundary where the backyard ends or the road narrows, diminishing out of sight...These paths are promises about where we might reach if we tried, if we kept, for instance, moving our pencils or tapping our word processor keys. Consciousness, I suggest, is in part defined by the way it always reaches beyond itself toward a fullness and a completeness that can never be attained. If it were attained, there would be a stoppage, a petrification. There would be no need for a quest.

It is my belief that when writing an essay, the writer must ask the reader to go on a quest for new knowledge, for new forms, for new answers, and most importantly, new questions, which is always a journey with no end in sight. Mere expertise in an idea or set of facts is always a "petrification" of the creative process. Instead, as poets and writers, it is our obligations to help our readers see the expansiveness of what their own imaginations can do.

It is with this spirit that my thinking about the poet's essay has originated. Maxine Greene also writes: "I am forever on the way." It is my task as a poet to show my readers that poets are always "forever on the way"—always ongoing, always en route to the next discovery, with each step taking us not closer to completion, but to a new beginning.

This book, I hope, will challenge some of your beliefs of what a poet's essay might or could be, and what it can do. I hope that you will begin to think of the concept of a poet's manifesto as something to be played around with and to begin to think of an Ars Poetica folding back within the essay form. I hope you will consider the notion of poetics not as a dry material but as a frame to hang ideas from and that the fantastic things our fantastic poets will bring to you in these essays will help you reconsider what a hybrid genre might mean. That it doesn't have to be a lens with which to market a piece of writing, but instead a formal gesture with the aesthetic logic of something like a poem at the forefront. Where the emergent truth is so much "better" than the projected or planned one. I hope that this book will make you think of things you couldn't have ever thought you might think about, and more.

Thank you for being here. Let's begin.

JUST CAPTIONS *Ariel Goldberg*

I. Subtextual Captions

I am drawn to captions, and notions of what a caption might mean poetically for photographic materials that remain vulnerable to losing their contextual information. Traces of identifying information are often in flux for trans and queer images of the late 20th century. The caption—if it exists at all—is an unstable clue, full of omission along with normative practice and language choices marked by their moment in linear time. But without the effort of a caption, how can people from different eras communicate—especially those who can't sit on a couch and look at photo albums together and speak the captions to each other?

I took a research picture of a small notebook while deep in the papers of photographer, filmmaker, activist Joan E. Biren (JEB) at the Sophia Smith Collection at Smith College in fall 2017. A brown 1970s font reads: Pocket Photo Notes and Negative Exposure Logbook over a dark yellow cover, with a faux leather texture. In the bottom right corner is a three-heading list for the notebook's owner to fill in, which JEB did with a faint black ballpoint pen: Book No.: One, Year: 1971-2, Camera: Nikomat.

Much more informative than the concise notes on f-stops and shutter speeds in the notebook were a dozen or so audio recordings from JEB's photography shoots from the late 1970s, which are digitized and available on site at the archives. She kept the cassette recorder on while conducting interviews during photographic sessions. She was making a book, the first to her knowledge, that would have the words "portraits" and "lesbian" in the title. JEB envisioned facing page captions, with selections of these interviews if the interviewee agreed, after reading the excerpted transcription. As the book developed, some people inside the pictures opted for no facing page text, and in that case, JEB ultimately included an excerpt of a poem she associated with the picture.

I listened to legs of light stands extended from their compact travel position; smooth metal descending to grip the floor. She asks rhetorically, "Is it too much equipment?" Thick shutter precedes an answer. To imitate the sound, I flop my tongue across the bridge of my mouth's suction; clack slurp. It just occurred to me apertures are like orifices. If you put a microphone next to even the softest, fastest sound it turns to jabs. Like I misread the tone of your message. Punctuation gone awry. In come the asterisks. Assumptions implode in gestures. Reverse, retreat. Comfort versus desire versus first impressions embedded in this routine of making images.

I translate the mechanism. Meanwhile I'm listening to the stiff air of people just getting to know each other. Pop of synchronized lights. Flash goes off, mixing with the natural light. Her film advances by a lever, getting to a new frame gives pause, advancements crunch, roll up, the darkness of inside the camera, along the grooves. She adjusts the shot, or repeats it, hoping for another facial expression to loosen up.

Nails of a dog's paw scratch against the wood floor following a kid into the room. The kid wants to know why there are silver umbrellas on stands, if it's not raining inside. "It makes the lights softer…it bounces on this umbrella, then it comes back and it's not so bright." The kid says, "oh," distrustful of her contraptions. Then she demos it. "It's still pretty bright," the kid says. I imagine the scene from JEB's archival records as if I am walking backwards, ready to bump into all the time passed when I was not there.

Eye to Eye: Portraits of Lesbians, Photographs by JEB 1979
by Joan E. Biren and Judith Schwarz

Paperback

$183.00 (9 used & new offers)

Making a Way Lesbians Out Front Jun 1, 1987
by Joan E. Biren

Paperback

$65.54 (15 used & new offers)

Figure 1: Screenshot (March 2018) of JEB's books as listed in an Amazon search. Thumbnails of book covers and pricing for used copies. *Eye to Eye: Portraits of Lesbians* (1979) listed at $183.00 and *Making a Way: Lesbians Out Front* (1987) listed at $65.54.

Back in my personal archive, the yellow glue of the book binding cracks as soon as I open my original copy of *Eye to Eye*. The pages become loose leaf in a manila envelope; I try to keep their order so the captions can match. JEB gifted me a rare copy of her book when we first met and I began researching her work. At the time of writing, *Eye to Eye* is out of print as well as *Making a Way*, her second book, both self-published under "Glad Hag Books" in 1979 and 1987 respectively.[1] In studying what's in the archival papers of a life's work, I bring my net of messy handwriting. I try to catch the marginalia of photography history's supposed margins.

---

1. In March 2021, Anthology Editions will release a reissue of Joan E. Biren's *Eye to Eye* for $30.

19

JEB turned to video after twenty years of making still photographs characterized by environmental portraits and protest documentation. In her early work, I search for the dialogue between her and her subjects in the correspondences, release forms, and rare cassette tape audio. All of a sudden the voices of the subjects are manifest in her documentary filmmaking because her new video camera quite literally recorded sound and image together.

I'm drawn in particular to JEB's video footage that got edited out of her various documentaries for its revelations of various contact between a person holding a camera and those who stand before it, willingly, or by accident. JEB's short and feature length documentaries either drew on home interviews with spokespeople of various LGBT organizations and cultural production across the country, or on conference panels from the 1990s and demonstrations.

It's 1992, at a New York City pride march, and someone on a loudspeaker is making an announcement for pink ribbons for a one-dollar donation, sized like they belong on a game of pin-the-tail-on-the-donkey. Light pink, not the blood red ribbon that crosses in a loop, that Visual AIDS began to popularize just one year earlier, which, in different colors, is the mainstream symbol of solidarity for a host of causes like mothers against drunk driving.

People JEB doesn't necessarily know in the crowd are "waving for the camera," perhaps a nervous tick to say I see you watching me. Meanwhile, the exhibitionist's photo release form resides in their leather thong. Someone with a t-shirt that reads "dyke" has a pair of pliers in her hands as she tries to finish making a pair of huge dangling disco ball earrings. She just can't get it, she says--I think--, "At least one is already in my other ear," as she bends over, her speech muffled. Barricades have not been rebranded over time; white stencils on periwinkle *it's-a-baby-boy!* blue: "do not cross." The New York Police Department is stationed firmly in the recorded image, hazarding against a full swing into nostalgia.

A leader of the dykes on bikes contingent is poised to unleash the first bundle of marchers. She comes to the front of the line with a cigarette glued to the wet envelope of her inner lip. She faces the other motorcyclists and a leafy green Central Park to the right. As if the conductor facing her orchestra, she tilts along her hunk of metal, signaling it's time to start. Her leather vest is unbuttoned for cleavage, short cut offs rubbing against her crotch. The revving of engines is uneven. Rows of vibrators on wheels, whoopee cushions amplified to a stadium audience. Their noise cancels out whatever excitement mixed with boredom JEB was picking up on camera. Questions are answered with questions: "Is it starting yet?" "Should we stand on this corner or that corner?"

I understand that this archival footage capturing the before or after, the in-between-the-events, all of what got cut from her final films as a crucial record of contact: unwritten captions in the pocket notebook.

The very process of creating image descriptions is also a tool to make images accessible to those who are not sighted, translate photographs into words. The life of the image on the screen benefits from unpredictable amounts of additive contextual information, an open call for the photo-album's narration, filled with free labor of captions writing from those whose memories can bend to the moment pictured.

II. Justice for the Caption

Figure 2: Screenshot of the online video documentation of a MoMA Forum on Contemporary Photography, "What Makes Contemporary Photography Feminist and Queer?" in January 2017. Projection of a black and white photograph of a group of people demonstrating at a gay pride parade in the early 1970s. A few heads of audience members near the bottom of the frame. A color miniature rectangle shows the video documentation of the panel discussion and audience at the forum.

The photo [figure 2] was one photo in the several photos the curator showed at the museum's discussion of "queer photography" that I was certain I had encountered and credited, while she claimed: "photographer unknown."

When I took a workprint of this Bettye Lane photo, [fig. 2], out of the plastic sheet, fitted for a three-ring binder, a New York Public library archivist walked over so swiftly to my station at the shared wooden table that her silk scarf began blowing in the air conditioning. She came to remind me about the rules of handling this collection, which included not photographing the materials. I let her know I was just looking for caption information on the back of the photo. I was wearing gloves. White fabric or were they latex? Perhaps she thought I was attempting to sneak a glare free cell phone photo of the original print.

When looking at the pencil marks of the backs of photos I look for identifying information for who is in the pictures. First name then a last name. Both maybe and sometimes. Was the photographer friends with those in the picture, just acquaintances? Were they known public figures? While I confirmed on my trip to the library that Bettye Lane took this picture, I learned she didn't record the names of the members of the Black Lesbian Caucus she photographed at this gay pride parade. A disappointment that is itself information. Who gave permission, maybe with a nod of recognition? Who did not consent? I especially ask these questions of a white photographer taking a picture of the Black Lesbian Caucus, which nearly fifty years later is presented by a white curator and now, again by me, a white poet-writer working through their research. At the time of presenting this talk in 2018 and still as I prepare it for publication in 2021, I am still looking to identify the people in this photo.

Who wanted their name attached to their image and who did not? What does an absence of names in the caption indicate about who the photographer took the photo for? Perhaps the desire to be recognized has changed. In the 1970s, there were not only fewer cameras around than today, but queer people, lesbians, often sought anonymity, especially if their images were reproduced in a way that would "out" them.

Figure 3: Screenshot of a lesbianherstoryarchives Instagram post (September 19, 2017) featuring a Paula Grant snapshot of Bettye Layne with a 35mm camera covering her face taking pictures at a meeting. Color photo of a white butch photographer kneeling in an educational setting of a dozen plus listeners around her; frame of image cuts off other people indicating a crowded room. Some femme presenting people sit on the floor others sit in school desks and table chairs. Two people in the picture acknowledge the photographer, Paula Grant capturing the moment. The caption for the image on Instagram commemorates Lane on her birthday, which is also the anniversary of her death (Sept 19,1930 - Sept 19, 2012). "[Lane was] one of the top news photographers of her time and one of the early documentarians of the feminist, and lesbian & gay rights movements. She was an early supporter of LHA and her work can be found here and in several other major archival collections." At the time of screenshot, there are 346 likes on the picture.

If my goal is to identify some or all the people in the photos I write about, then how to find people in a crowd? How does a crowd, a public space, a demonstration shift the focus of attention away from individuals? What about influential political formations and collectives within crowds? How to then return to an individual among histories of collectives?

I also remember seeing Lane's photo [fig. 4] lean in a picture frame one could buy at a pharmacy on a bookshelf at the Lesbian Herstory Archives (LHA) in Brooklyn, relatively exposed to the elements, of dust, foot traffic from book sales, sweat collecting on drinks at public events, meetings about meetings starting on time; at one archive you can't take pictures of the pictures, but at another you can photocopy the pictures—not for reproduction, but for research. Inconsistencies dance in my notes.

Figure 4: Screenshot of a lesbianherstoryarchives photo posted February 6, 2018. Six Black femme-presenting and gender non-conforming people in the foreground of the crowd directly face the photographer and her camera. One holds a balloon, another sips from a can of soda, two hold signs. One sign reads "BLACK LESBIAN CAUCUS," another "The Blacker the Berry, the Sweeter the Dyke." In the background a huge cloth banner with the words "Lesbians Unite." A white woman in the background also faces the camera holding a sign "Love Unites." Many hold balloons with an illegible phrase stenciled on them.

The LHA posted a version of Lane's photo in their collection and here I encounter a third possible date for this photo. On the front bottom margin of the print, "1973," is handwritten next to Lane's name. Looking at the back of yet another copy of the photo, this one found in Lane's collection at the New York Public Library, this time I find the date 6-24-71, which also differs from the curator's caption date of 1972. In her caption to the Instagram post for Figure 4, LHA Coordinator and Photo Archivist Saskia Scheffer provides context to the history and evolution of the Black Lesbian Caucus, but does not begin identifying people in the picture. Scheffer quotes (from Wikipedia) early collective member Candice Boyce: at the time of the group's founding, "there was no other place for women of color to go and sit down and talk about what it means to be a black lesbian in America."

The people's names in this Bettye Lane picture from 1971-73 *appear* lost in a photographer's archives within a library's manuscript and archives division or even further lost within an art world deeply rooted in white supremacy and heterosexism. But their names are not lost. I'm learning now through the research and writing of Shawn(ta) Smith-Cruz about the history of The Black Lesbian Caucus of the New York City Gay Activist Alliance. It became Salsa Soul Sisters in 1974, a group for African American Lesbians, also open to Asian American, Latina, and Native American women and those along the gender spectrum. In 1976, the group incorporated as Third World Wimmin. Early members of Salsa Soul Sisters included Candice Boyce, Reverend Delores Jackson, Betty "Achebe" Jean Powell, Maua Flowers, Harriet Austin, Sonia Bailey, and Luvenia Louise Pinson—but I am still working to figure out *who specifically* is in this photo.

Transition of Salsa Soul Sisters archival materials began with a donation to LHA by Georgia Brooks in 1983 and continued in 2016 when Salsa Soul Sisters members Cassandra Grant, Imani Rashid, Nancy Valentine, and Brahma Curry worked with Smith-Cruz to process this collection. As LHA continues to produce metadata for this collection, Smith-Cruz meets with Salsa Soul members to collectively caption the hundreds of photographs in the Salsa Soul archives. Smith-Cruz has in recent years curated an exhibition based on the Salsa Soul Sisters archival materials that has traveled to the EFA Robert Blackburn Printmaking Workshop Program, Brooklyn College's Library to The Studio Museum in Harlem, and the New York Historical Society. Salsa Soul Sisters eventually became African Ancestral Lesbians United for Social Change (AALUSC), which is active today.

What first appeared to me as an absence of names was really an absence of context: the gulf between the fact of grassroots Black lesbian collectives and photographic, curatorial, and institutional practices that do not devote themselves to retaining information around the images they circulate. I've inherited processes of erasure that call for the slow work of inquiry—not only for what appears missing but how it came to appear lost in the first place.

How to incorporate the lived and material differences between photographers and those in their pictures, between photographic norms and practices across time—what norms do I perform or stumble to reject as a poet approaching writing where attention to detail in these histories means building trust and relationships?

III. Endurance of Errata

In Fall 2017, I read a pamphlet available to visitors of the two-part "interwoven" exhibitions "A Recollection. + Predicated." at the Kitchen in NYC, curated by Tiona Nekkia McClodden. The exhibitions were part of the larger project "Julius Eastman: That Which is Fundamental," a multi-artist and venue series presenting Eastman's scores in concert events, co-curated with Dustin Hurt, presented both Philadelphia and New York City. The exhibition "A Recollection." presented a historical exhibit of Eastman considering his life and work as a gay African-American composer and performer featuring archival materials; the companion exhibition "Predicated.," (on view on the same floor as "Recollection.") featured 14 contemporary artists who are "steeped in notions of absence, trace presence, duration, and the politics of exhaustion." As a group show, "Predicated." both "illuminates and is illuminated by Eastman's legacy."[2] Inside the pamphlet, McClodden says to Ladi'Sasha Jones, in an interview,

> The weakest part of this exhibit is the limited presence of Eastman's voice articulating who he was and his own conceptual practice. I have told all of the artists to consider the fact that this could also happen to you and such is the importance of writing and speaking about their own work. Eastman's press coverage, while pretty steady during his Buffalo years, was not primarily focused on speaking with him—it was interested in talking about him and his music. That's a phenomenon that is replicated across the art world today, where you have more people talking about you than are talking to you. And things are put in print that becomes your legacy.

Much of McClodden's work addresses this risk of absence and misrepresentation that Eastman faced. McClodden does this by setting up long-term projects, making the space and time for research and intergenerational dialogue between Black queer artists.

Around the time I went to "A Recollection. + Predicated." I signed a contract with a glossy contemporary art magazine for a feature essay about the sudden focus of the MoMA Forums on Contemporary Photography on "queer photography." The essay took up the question: what happens when a bastion of institutional photography acts like it is discovering work it had intentionally ignored for decades? The piece began with trying to make sense of the Lane photograph of the Black Lesbian Caucus. While I finished that essay, I am still (in 2022) researching this image.

The contract asks art writers to avoid writing about artists they know or have a relationship with. To avoid conflicts of interest, the contract also asks you not to show the writing to the artists you are writing about

---

2. https://www.tionam.com/juliuseastman

before publication. But I wish I signed an opposite contract, one that specified I had to check that I represented the work accurately with the (living) artists I was writing about. The contract I signed makes a fictional mist of art writing as being exempt from self-portrait. Interpretations are not so easy to fact check. The artist speaking about their work refuses the distance, distortion, and loss to art criticism. They challenge mainstream narratives and familiar canons. Ideally, there would be plenty of informed, well-researched writing from people with a range of personal familiarity to the artists' work, as well as the artists speaking for themselves.

I have long been obsessed with the "Corrections" section in journalism. And I am trying to figure out what it might have to do with lost captions. What do we come to understand as a single error as opposed to a whole set of norms within art writing or journalism? What happens when an error that lives in material online is updated but the trace of the correction becomes lost? How can we preserve more of the process?

> Blind spots make themselves legible:

> Correction: September 17, 2017, An article on Page 16 this weekend about the growing prominence of gender-fluid artists refers incorrectly to Diamond Stingily, an artist. Ms. Stingily is not transgender. The article also refers incorrectly to Sadie Benning's series of photographs. They are portraits, but not self-portraits.

Hilarie M. Sheets, in her article "Gender-Fluid Artists Come Out of the Gray Zone" had assumed that an artist in the exhibition was transgender who is not and that another artist who does identify as transgender was making self-portraits, but they are portraits. From this documented correction, we receive a record also of the art writer's assumptions and the wavering durability of one of the most reputable newspapers in this country to fact-check. I write a letter to the editor after encountering the article and the correction.

> The crux of Hilarie M. Sheets "Gender-Fluid Artists Come

Out of the Gray Zone is a direct quote from artist Juliana Huxtable: "...the policing and the violence against trans people have a direct relationship to [this] increase in visibility." The New York Times must heed Huxtable's words and examine the responsibility that comes with celebrating The New Museum's exhibition Trigger, opening next week. In addition to claiming the relevancy of this exhibition to a vague political climate and representations of trans people on television, the Times has a duty to more consistently cover the epidemic of transwomen of color being murdered, criminalized, and harassed at record high rates. 21 transgender and gender non-conforming people have been lost in 2017 so far to homicide. Where is the story in the Times about Derricka Banner's murder, the last Transwoman to fall in this epidemic? I commend the Times for publishing an op-ed by Jamal Lewis on her personal stakes in this emergency, but we need more consistent coverage, otherwise ignorance will continue to try to destroy us.

Thomas Feyer, The Times's letters editor. Stephen Hiltner/The New York Times

Figure 5: Screenshot of Thomas Feyer, The New York Times's letters editor. Photo by Stephen Hiltner. A white man turns to face camera and smiles, seated at his desk in a cubicle overloaded with books. His hands rest on a mouse and keyboard, his computer is out of view.

The editor didn't print my letter in response to Sheet's article. I wonder if an unpublished letter can count as a lost caption. I take a screenshot of my original email to make an image of the one-sided correspondence. There are too many letters to respond to personally, the *Times* does warn you in an automatic reply, preparing you for the likelihood your letter will not be published. But the letter to the editor doesn't quite fall through the cracks, it bounces back up on that trampoline of restless poetic matter, ready to be melted down and repurposed for the next thought process.

ANTIWEST OR THE BEGINNING   *Ken Chen*

Antiwest or The Beginning

In the A was the word
Let A be "Beginning"
Let A be Alpha and Alphabet and Aleph Let A be see
(ing all creation from a lone point)
The —, eph
emera
His metamorphosis into ephemera
His metamorphosis not effable
If this end formed an origin
Let A be the sea
You buried him above the giant hole called ocean
In what hole universe have you been birthed
If you are a writer
In the beginning was the word

What is a beginning?

This is the book of the generations from the West and from the rest spoken from a voice from a void from a place of rest, so many races and peoples and species brought forth, limbs and babies and bodies birthed and fruited, spores of generations first and second seeding genus, class, logical collection, the race of reason across the man-age. And the beginning was tohu wa bohu. What we saw upon the surface of the deep was darkness.

What is the darkness?

Was this chaos what Anaximander named Arkhe, the limitless principle prior to even the heavens and the cosmos? When I read about this substance, I thought of Mare Tenebroso, the Sea of Darkness that the late Medievals believed to shroud Africa, whose center lay as secret from the Europeans who could only imagine white sanctuary hidden there, white jewels glinting from the palaces of the pious Prester John, who ruled an interior empire of gems and crystals, giants and centaurs, this Christian potentate inspired by Orientalist fantasies, but who symbolized a promised cavalry that would save the crusaders from the forces of Islam. The Europeans still believed that Prester John existed even in the Seventeenth and Eighteenth Centuries as Portuguese ships tacked their sails against the wind of another world.

What is Portugal?

The knights want to wage crusade and so the knights sail from England but along the way the knights say why not let's do it, let's pillage Spain and thus: Portugal.

What is a beginning?

A few days after it happened the three of us came down
    the hill.
I mean myself my sister and my stepmother.
We clutched yellow dollar bills and blue dollar bills.
Dollar bills issued by the Federal Reserve Bank of Hell.
We stopped a thousand feet from home.
My stepmother laid our cauldron onto the asphalt.
We stuffed sheets of 世界日報 into the cauldron.
We lit the newspapers.
The tapered lighter's flame weak like a tear.
We said nothing.
We held the hell money.
We were mourning solitudes.
We dipped the hell money into the flames.
The flames first tentative and then vehemently engorged.
The gluttonous flames.
The flames hot enough to dry our tears.
This is when.
This is when our neighbors came.

Our neighbors came wearing sunglasses and moved
    with the curious leisure of those on vacation,
    though they were simply returning home.

Our neighbors came perhaps noting to themselves,
    These people have erected a bonfire on our driveway.
Perhaps our neighbors categorized this as atypical
    suburban behavior.
Our neighbors knew this was where he died.
We noted them.
We cried without self-awareness.
We stuffed more bills into the vessel's hot music.
Note after note.
Heaps of hell money.
We took on faith that the flames sublimated the dollars
    into the next world.
Wire transfers to inferno.
We cried.
And this is when one of the neighbors spoke.
One of the neighbors said she saw him.
He had been driving down the hill when she saw him
    coast into the shoulder where he braked and
    slumped forward into the steering wheel.
Was this too much information?
Did I want to think this image?
Did I want to think this image?

What is twilight?

When we burnt money to send to hell that late afternoon, I saw the sun decline into the early white evening and sink into what our ancestors had called *hesperos* or *vesper*. These words engendered another word: the "west." For does not the sun soak into the night at its western point?

What is the West?

In 1503, Columbus found himself stranded in Jamaica, where his men were initially welcomed and given food by the Taino until that matriarchal tribe betrayed those who imagined themselves to be their benefactors. Relying on a prediction of an upcoming lunar eclipse, Columbus supposedly admonished the Taino that their god would inflame the moon to punish them for not aiding Columbus and his men. When the indigenous men saw the moon redden in the sky, according to Columbus's son, they let out a "great howling and lamentation" and "came running from every direction to the ships, laden with provisions, praying the Admiral to intercede by all means with God on their behalf." (It should be noted that our only record of this is a self-aggrandizing source: Columbus's own diary.) This trope—the superstitious native cowering before celestial fate and Western rationality—makes frequent appearances in colonial literature from H. Rider Haggard's *King Solomon's Mines* to *Tin Tin* comics. When Prospero himself retires from his lofty heights as mage-auteur in Shakespeare's *Tempest*, explicitly releasing Ariel from bondage but not necessarily Caliban, he lists the powers he will relinquish, one of them being the ability to "bedim... / the noontide sun." In a counter-parody, the Honduran/Guatemalan writer Augusto Monterroso imagines a Spanish friar who threatens that he will blot out the sun if indigenous tribesmen attack him. The natives kill him anyways. They have already predicted the eclipse using Mayan astronomy. These stories deploy the eclipse to suggest Western mastery over both Dionysian primitives and the Apollonian heavens, but there lays repressed within the image a more accurate subtext. What hungry womb swallowed the sun? Walk West, where the world ends.

What is the Atlantic?

If he disembarked not from Spain or Italy but from
    west Africa, that Italian captain
If this is what writers refer to as foreshadowing
If the Santa Maria and the Niña and the Pinta were
    smaller than tennis courts
If he piloted from "dead reckoning," navigating against
    his past like an animal
If soon they saw naked people
If the people were well-built and strong
If I saw their good bodies and handsome features
If I displayed my sword and one of them, not knowing
    what it was, grabbed it by the blade
If in return, he cupped in his bloody palms, a parrot
If the bird's green feathers caressed my hand, such
    strange comfort after these months at sea
If I thought to myself that with fifty men we could

    subjugate them all
If the people were nude of immunity
If we forgot we made homes where the maggot ate
If you gasped when you learned the number was 100
    million
If you did not know that death had undone so many
If the arteries of these ghosts drifted into the rock
If a ghost is what we call history minus body
If the wound where we drew the silver from their veins
    was called Potosi
If you read about the gold and silver of the dead
    continents, the "entombment in mines of the
    aboriginal population," as the first item on a list
If the second item of the list was the conquest and
    looting of the East Indies
If you read the last item: the "turning of Africa into a
    warren for the commercial hunting of black-skins"
If this genesis list consisted of a syllogism, if this
    colonial alpha signaled the "rosy dawn of
    capitalist production" for a young political
    economist named Karl Marx
Rosy dawn of that sun, the Death Star
In the beginning was the word
If the West was when the night began
Night = End ≠ Beginning = Antiwest
In the antiwest was the word
In the beginning was the word
If Beginning, Arkhe, means Archive
In the archive was the word

Ergo Antiwest = Archive
But the West invented the Archive (West = Archive)
Ergo Antiwest = Word = Archive = West
Ergo Antiwest = West
ERROR!
WRONG!
If your father was a man
If she tries to snuggle, you commit genocide
If you commit genocide, you are bad man
To say the least!
If three years later your infant on your chest does doze
If all men are mortal
WRONG!
If your father is a man
WRONG!
If your father was a man
What does it mean to say the least
We call the first and second sentences false conditionals
1 No causal link btwn snuggling & genocide Please proceed to snuggle
2 Logical syllogisms cannot create moral value
If you commit genocide, you must be imagining things
If you are genocide imagining things, you may be what
    the West calls romanticism
If you are imagining things, you are still not a zombie
If your spirit evacuates your zombie body, there may
    be reasons
If what happened was beyond reason
To say the least!

What does it mean to say the least?

If to say the least is: Reason
If mathematics like money and markets summon zero
    morality
If all persons must make their way to an end
If an end means both purpose and termination
If empire is a name for administering the ends of
    persons
If syllogism extends a ruse of comprehension
If syllogism implies what happened was reasonable
If modus ponens suborns us into carceral recursion
If what we wanted was a world as small as comprehension
If all we are left with are words and the dead

What is wrong?

A wrong is a line in space that has been placed atop another line in space. A latter is when we climb one wrong after another wrong and find ourselves late.

What is late?

You are belated if you lag behind a colonial power. You are late if you are recently dead
and a proper noun.
Related beloved belated relation:
The late Simon Chen.

THE CHEERFUL SCAPEGOAT *Wayne Koestenbaum*

Crocus was the first to appear at the party. She wore a dress designed by Adolph Gottlieb—a frock checkered with pictographs. Within its antic designs, she'd seek cognitive replenishment. And yet her doctor had warned, "Don't turn to inanimate patterns for emotional gratification." Thus Crocus had decided to break her monastic vow and attend the party. Crocus, upon entering the townhouse, hid in the vestibule. She studied the pictographs on her dress. Would these conical, intersecting shapes provide a road map for the evening? Would circles and X's and arrows, arranged with a glee practically catatonic in its excess, decode the arcane niceties of her fellow partygoers? Crocus cowered beside umbrellas and overcoats in the dim vestibule, a pathway to a party that her doctor (whom she categorized as a "miscreant- confessor") had aggressively urged her to attend.

"I won't enter the party," thought Crocus. "I will telephone my miscreant-confessor. Certainly he will give me advice."

What happened to Crocus's good cheer? Wasn't she still fantasizing about summers by the lake—humid idylls from someone else's childhood, not her own?

We will skip over the rest of the party. Other narrative duties await us, and Crocus has grown unappealing as a focus of dismay. Our dismay, an ermined entity, needs larger sway than Crocus can provide.

Suddenly remorseful for having abandoned Crocus in the vestibule, we return to her plight and decide to pose as the telephoned miscreant-confessor, to whom Crocus had placed, just a moment ago, a call intercepted by this ham-fisted voice we currently occupy, lacking another voice to articulate the distance between abstraction and figuration in the war-game rooms where decisions about nuclear eventualities are broached and bartered.

A half-hour of animated conversation commenced, on a cell phone, between the miscreant-confessor and Crocus, who took shelter in phrases that we, posing, dispensed. The miscreant-confessor then vanished, and Crocus made short work of the party. Newly bold in her Adolph Gottlieb dress, she sauntered from clique to clique.

"Do you want to see the host's bedroom?" asked a fashionable mortician whom Crocus had befriended. Crocus took the mortician's hand, and the two friends walked down a hallway to a door left ajar. Pushing open the door, Crocus walked toward the bed. The mortician refused to follow Crocus into the room; the mortician had a narrowness of viewpoint considered a sine qua non of artistic skill in earlier centuries, though her tendency to truncate every vista into a still life deprived her of the boldness required to be an effective companion and chaperone of Crocus, whose lability and chromophobia placed her in pickle after pickle, a "domino effect" of faux pas, from which she would need to be extricated by a companion exclusively committed to Crocus's weal.

Deprived of chaperone, Crocus stood over the bed, where a woman was lying on top of a man. Both were mostly clothed, though there were significant absences of habiliment, patches of disorganized skin showing through shirt-flap and pajama-fissure. The woman, who had, a moment ago, draped her body on top of the man, raised herself and stood beside Crocus. Together, this woman and Crocus looked down at the man, who remained face up; something unformed and infantile about his features provoked, in Crocus, a spasm of revulsion, as if she were looking at a Chardin painting for the first time and were not comprehending her ecstasy—a conundrum which forced Crocus to shove her rapture into a different medicine-cabinet, a hiding-place christened "Disgust."

"I've finished blowing him," said the woman to Crocus, "and now he's virtually lifeless, a passive slob, dreaming of unsolvable equations."

"Do you regret blowing him?" asked Crocus, newly enamored of this woman, because of her suave way of jettisoning responsibility for the man whom she had blown.

"I don't yet know you," said the woman, whose name, Crocus would momentarily learn, was Jesse, "but something neutral and flat in your demeanor suggests that we might together form an army."

"An army of two?" asked Crocus, already tired of being relegated to the position of meek questioner.

"I have other soldiers at my disposal," said Jesse, enigmatically brushing the hair away from her sweaty forehead.

The man on the bed woke from his stupor, and said, "Jesse, introduce me to your new friend."

"I don't yet know her name, though she seems to know mine," said Jesse.

"Crocus," volunteered the newest member of this bedroom's army.

"Pleased to meet you, Crocus," said the man on the bed, whom we will nominate as the miscreant-confessor in a new, prone, blown guise.

The hall-of-mirrors sensation overwhelmed Crocus again, as she tried to sort out the dramatis personae in the bedroom. "Am I a judge?" wondered Crocus. "Or am I a colonel in a tiny militia? Or am I simply a partygoer who stumbled into the wrong room, and should quickly exit, before I lose control of myself?"

The party's host barged in. "Hello, friends! What rebel convocation are you spoilsports forming, behind my back?"

Many years ago, before the political catastrophe that now threatened the nation, Crocus had loved the host, a tomboy named Taddeo. Once a Theodora, later a Tad, and finally a Taddeo, the host survived on the hefty earnings that came to her through sacrificial channels, sub-legal, sub-rosa, sub-material. The sub-materiality of Taddeo's sacrifices—rituals that harmed only the spirit but left unmolested the body—accrued interest through clandestine and reputedly aqueous transactions, which gave her the resources to throw legendary parties, each of them featuring a new sacrifice.

Crocus, of course, was this party's secret sacrifice. Crocus knew it, everyone knew it. Only the miscreant-confessor did not know, and that ignorance is why the miscreant-confessor dimwittedly forced Crocus to attend the party. So sectarian and convoluted were the workings of Crocus's destiny, we are surprised that she had enough pluckiness and composure to put on the Adolph Gottlieb dress without ripping it in the process of pulling the too-tight sheath over her head and attempting to slither the uncomfortable rayon over a body that no longer wished to accommodate a dead artist's pictographs.

"And now it is my turn to lie down on the foul bed," said Crocus.

"No," said Taddeo. "The sacrifice that pertains to you is happening later tonight, in the music room."

"Beside the harpsichord?" asked Crocus. Who in this metropolis did *not* know about the notorious harpsichord of Taddeo MacRae?

"Are you afraid of my harpsichord?" asked Taddeo.

"Of course Crocus is," grumbled Jesse. "Fool she'd be, not to fear an instrument designed to tangle up the minds of everyone within hearing range."

The amorphous and unnamed man on the bed, whom many in the army had typecast as the enemy, was in fact a distant descendant of Chardin. The refinement of the keen-eyed ancestor had trickled down to the man on the bed, who saw the situation around him with a lucidity that permitted him to realize that all perspective lines converged on the cone-like consciousness of Crocus. The man on the bed wiped his mouth, to free his powers of articulation from the imaginary impediment that slobber represented to a paranoid orgiast.

"Tomorrow night," Crocus said, "I fly to Nice."

"No," said the man on the bed. "No," said Taddeo. "No," said Jesse. Each "no" sounded rehearsed; the pitch of each negation was eschatologically precise, without tremor.

Instantly, Crocus gave up her plans to walk down the Promenade des Anglais. She gave up her plans to take movement classes at the hotel. She would find a movement studio here in town. She would begin movement classes the next day, if she survived the party, if the still unscripted events, destined to take place that night around the harpsichord, left her sufficiently unscarred.

"What kinds of movements am I attempting to learn?" thought Crocus. The answer didn't matter. Most important was to *plan* to learn how to move in a new way, even if these newly baptized methods had no basis in medical or spiritual fact.

"I will begin my movement classes tomorrow morning," Crocus murmured, later that evening, as she stood beside the harpsichord—the circle of partygoers surrounding the instrument and the sacrifice. "I will learn how to move like a swan. Or like a tugboat. Or like an iguana." Taddeo and Jesse smiled at Crocus, who was a good learner.

Rameau's ornamentation posed difficulties for the harpsichordist, a local hack, who lacked knowledge of period styles. The harpsichordist's mordents were clumsy, and Crocus felt stung by their maladroitness. The harpsichordist, who could no doubt sense Crocus's dismay, placed that dismay on a distant shelf in a clavier-consciousness whose only duty, tonight, lay in the parsimoniously shaped phrase, the intrusively plangent appoggiatura, the strategically irregular trill.

To leave Crocus now, in her circle of flagellants, at the mercy of a crude harpsichordist and a thrill-hungry group of behavior-experimentalists, shows no cruelty on our part. Our sympathies lie with Crocus. We admire her cheerfulness. She brings mirth and contrast to the monochromatic, humorless rooms through which she passes, on her slow journey toward tomorrow's movement classes, taught by incompetent masters with no grasp of kinetic fundamentals, and no tenderness for the bodies whose flesh is subject to the palpations and distensions of movement-sages without scruple. We admire the movement teachers, despite their unethical haggardness. "Tomorrow I will find a new way to move," Crocus continued to murmur. The harpsichordist ignored her senseless mutterings. A good instrumentalist must pay strict attention to the tempo. Without a steady yet flexible pulse, the piece approaches ruin. Ruin might be a good goal, however, if Crocus's sufferings are to be our guide. Crocus's consciousness burned down to the slimmest filament of plausibility. And yet its flame continued to attract flagellants and admirers. Around Crocus, the admirers stayed fast within their circle formation. The admirer-flagellants held hands, to keep the circle serene and firm. Crocus began to dance—if you call those stumbling steps a dance. The movement class was already in process, and it had no teacher. "I am already where tomorrow told me I must wait for it to arrive," Crocus said, in a loud, clear voice. Her dance-collapse, a cross between resurrection and ruin, attained a new fixity and vividness. "This dance is where we must now live," she continued, in her bright confident tone. She staggered and regained balance and staggered again. The circle of flagellant-admirers clapped their hands rhythmically, with a ferocity veined by igneous strands of kindness. To call our behavior *kind*—to call this congregation *civilized*—requires an imagination addicted to the fumes that rise from notoriety. Who is notorious tonight? Crocus is newly notorious, and will remain so as long as she continues to carve out, through non-movement, a movement class without master. Now we must efface this sordid investigation by rubbing a turpentine-soaked rag over the figure's already smeared features.

POETRY, THE BODY, MANIFESTO
Tracie Morris

It is a great pleasure to muse with this panel on relating poetry and the poetic imagination to the essay and manifesto. My new book, *Who Do With Words*, is called a manifesto because I wanted to be clear about its advocacy, its subjectivity, its passion. It's semi-autobiographical and about philosopher J.L. Austin, Blerdom and Black power. This essay is about it, me, my process in writing my first "essay" book, and what I hope to achieve in this fledgling effort.

This book was tough to write because it makes plain some of the more subtly worded raisons d'être for my writing poems, essays and now this new thing.

As my seventh written or edited book, I hope it's lucky. As embodiment, it's my heart on my sleeve. It's my heart on my arm without covering my pulse.

As the first part of a triptych of writings on J.L. Austin, I can't help but frame this conversation as a trinity too: Heart, Mind, Spirit. Manifesto, Essay, Poem. I am, of course, making up these categories. They are interchangeable and none of them is real. Their constructions, like race, gender and time, are human made and yet, because we act on these constructions, the implications, the perlocutions, are real.

1

Let's try this again: Heart, Mind, Spirit: Locution, Illocution, Perlocution. Imma let me finish: Meaning, Intent, Effect. Once more: What I feel, manifesto; what I think, essay; what the results are, the poem.

These three categories, this three-card monty does not, of course, offer an order. This is non-linear.

I've gone over several drafts in my comments today and that means tossing and turning, not watching and watching tv, eating and not eating, worrying.

I think we're all worried and worry as academics: we overthink and we overkill. How many drafts of a dissertation? How many drafts of a paper? What's this draft like? Boy was it drafty yesterday.

In *How To Do Things with Words*, J.L. Austin permutes on the word "mean," as in meaning, about three times: meaning in terms of definition, in terms of intention, in terms of effect. "What he really meant was..." to contrast what actually happened. What J.L. Austin does not do is refer to "mean" as cruelty. Probably why I like him.

The ellipses expression: "I mean..." is a search for the middle, for this balance. I realized this morning that there was embedded in all this, the "golden mean." Between poetry and manifesto is the essay. So I guess this is what this commentary I'm saying now is.

2

This essay refers to a manifesto based on poems. The poems seek to concentrate, to articulate the primary human knowing through utterance of the extraordinary. The manifesto seeks to articulate passion, explicating the mundane. So what is this essay?

As *How To Do Things With Words* offers, there isn't one right answer. Only categories that get us closer to what we mean. This essay became an explanation of a book I wrote you haven't read (yet?).

As it was raining outside yesterday, I remembered the performance Derek Jacobi did as Lear at BAM a couple years ago. He whispered the "Blow winds blow" monologue. He chose to perform it in secret. Being Jacobi, it could be heard in the pin-drop clarity of the back of the house.

The poetics of dramatic poetry is to amplify and silence the wind. To harness this element, reminded me of what the poem cannot do: it cannot "mean" anything. An essay's purpose is to mean something. In this case to serve as a "mean" between poem and manifesto.

— but not to be mean, which a manifesto or poem can do, what I have done in poems and in this manifesto book, maybe, but that was not its intention. Not what I mean.

3

Writing my first manifesto is/was difficult because I didn't want to appear to be mean even if my effort to be meaningful, hurt feelings. Will those feelings be hurt? I'm putting out feelers in this essay.

I realize that what I want, what most if not all people want is joy, is happiness — and one tries not to reach for this at anyone else's expense. This is what I go through all the time trying to say different things in different contexts (poem, essay, manifesto) rather than other things (singing, acting, professing).

Happiness as a construct, as a meaning, is vague, and J.L. Austin makes it vaguer in his book by talking about speech performances that don't work, as unhappy or infelicitous. He talks about being unhappy more than being happy, about failure more than success, and I guess I'm doing that too.

Don't we do that? Isn't that what academia is about? Brooding? I feel that our predisposition to show smarts is encapsulated in the speech act: "yeah but..." I do this too. Sometimes in poems, essays, and songs. I wonder where this disposition might come from. For me it feels like a disengagement with the body. "You're always in your head." I've said to myself more than once. It may or may not have been said about me behind my back. When said behind my back, it's outside. When said to myself, where is it?

4

In my sound poetry the answer is viscera. In my poetic imagination, the meaning is clearly acting "inside out." Vibrate the organs, the breathing ones, to touch the ones in you to go beyond literal meaning and into the indescribable transcendent and universal sound pitch. The omnitexts that vibrate everything. Out of one's head, out of one's "mind" is where the poetic imagination resides in some way. The body is taken into account with the physics of poetics. What I'm seeking in the essay that's harder to get to in that form, is embodied practice, embodied statements that are not constative because they reverberate (and J.L. Austin says that this is what all statements do when they do things — which they all do — and that's why constative ultimately fails: reverberation is doing). Reverberation is the uttering body's permission to speak for itself.

But what of the speaking of others? This particular inhabited body is constated as female, Black, short, African-American, Brooklynish, grown, bookish, dreadlocked. Do I look like a poet, an academic? A sibling, someone's child? A scholar? Someone's teacher? The embodiment works in and out and I guess when I say I wear my heart on my sleeve, on my arm, in a manifesto book I mean the viscera is outside of me, but can it live there? Is it, in another Jacobean role, "Vic(i)ous?"

Maybe sometimes on the outside. On the inside I'm always trying to get at that "thing." Some call it "that music." Whatever it is, it's poetic. I'm reaching in and out, up and down, through and through.

5

All these efforts engage the senses, to reference Susan Stewart's book. When one is not saying words, when one bypasses the heart, if you will, of the constative, one gets to the heart of the performative, hopefully or at least the arm or sleeve of the performative. The poem is the synecdoche of language rather than the etiolation of language. This is where J.L. Austin and I disagree.

Outside of the chest the heart can be harmed but we also see how red it is, how it beats. In the manifesto one could say the same thing but we usually, when exposed to righteous stridency, say: "That took guts." Less glamorous and smellier than the heart sometimes, but showing the unpleasant insides without equivocation is what is intended, the illocution of that statement.

The intention of *Who Do With Words* is to reach a more mainstream Black audience and to make things plain, to tell a few truths. Less poetics and more exposure, less for academics but more for non-academic Black nerds and others. Socialized female, I don't want to "hurt feelings," and that often gets us into female trouble. Gut-wrenching is what I would call this book (wrenching my own guts) and therefore it is much like sound poetry in the way it feels in me, a self-reverberating perlocutionary aspect. Rather than performing its effect to others, this manifesto book reveals my feelings to myself as part of interacting groups of others. Who is doing the thing and what the thing is that's doing something with identity and unequivocal meaning, assertion.

Divorced from the primary impulse toward economy, as I am in page-based poetry and to an extent sound poetry, the manifesto's plaintive nature and this essay's attempt to explain are anti-(aes)thetical to my poetic tendencies and therefore this manifesto is

6

freeing. It attempts to assert the freedom of others like me. Whereas a poem can emphasize ways to not speak, this essay I'm speaking now is saying a whole bunch of things, none of which is implied.

One way I am understanding what essays do is to go in the polar opposite direction of what I'd like to do as a poet with the same idea. A manifesto is making an assertion, and that is also not what I'm doing right now, in this essay. It is not a "force" in that way, or the way that J.L. Austin uses forces either, it's an offering of an idea as a series of statements of some type. It is stream of consciousness in flow as the autonomy of self that automatic writing is, improvised in tap-tap touch type in my conceptual pecking order.

To riff on the current Black behabitive, "What I'm not gonna do is…" use my manifesto to dominate, hopefully, but to assert/ascertain (if I'm trying to do anything in it), in this preface to it in my comments for this forum. The book manifesto is to assert empowerment without repression and with passion. I wrote *Who Do with Words* as a manifesto on Black freedom. We do this in many non-Austinian ways, including song as manifesto like the ring shout. It "rings out." Although not the etymology of the term, the ring shout uses the pacing, the pulsing syncopation to reverberate and if there is metal and glass in the room, that includes "ringing."

The manifesto reverberates through passion rather than through sound— or at least it does for me in this first effort. The targeted audience of Blerds (Black nerds) later includes others of good will. The focus of the book for Black audiences is a form of performance to find the golden mean in myself too.

7

This essay is a preface, as I said. I think about being a Blackademic (and here we are formatted in the Ivy Leagues today). In the academy the intimacy of being the right person in the right environment with the right credentials and that usually means being acceptable in the right social environments.

I investigate that construct as a way of balancing the perception outside of my body about who I am. I assert my fundamental self pre-academy and pre-avant-garde core: as a sickly baby Blerd in the projects with my Blerdy sibling, our early meanings and sounds before my adoption into other less-Black contexts that have embraced me.

We on the margins are always re-introducing ourselves sometimes outing ourselves sometimes saying what we mean by what we appear to as others.

In a couple days when *Who Do With Words* is ready to be seen, maybe some of this may make sense, maybe it won't. This commentary is what is on my mind and I realized that I want to be happy to convey happiness/felicity and, as I said in the introduction to another book, "universal love and care for everyone." That's what the book is about even though that's not necessarily what it "gives off." What I have learned as a poet is to accept what the writing means, whether or not that is what I "want" it to mean.

8

There is a higher intention besides being liked, being acceptable. It's telling the truth as best as one can. One facet of it with passion, asserting what is meaning-full. A manifesto.

Here I talk about J.L. Austin's speech act theory through aspects of Black power through Blerd culture. I wrote this book because the traditional academic post-thesis "book" did not serve my passion for the project. It felt too "square." So instead I'm creating 3 books: One on heart (this first one), one for mind (the second one) and one for spirit (the more open-ended third).

The first book is embodiment but through an ephemeral symbol: the heart. The heart is the core of the manifesto.

Looking outside myself, I again considered the Abomunist Manifesto by Bob Kaufman and African Signs and Spirit Writing by Harryette Mullen. One's a "poem" and one's an "essay," but I feel that they both reflect the best that manifestos can be because they both express passion in speaking truth to power, with wry wit on top of everything, something I cannot claim, but aspire to.

Almost all our work, as Black poets, as marginalized people, is political because our embodiment makes these words mean particular things, they inhabit us and reflect us and therefore embody our particular situation: that is, we are affirming ourselves to ourselves while simultaneously being "forced"—that word again—to prove our fundamental human nature, our existence, to others. It is always being questioned by those who have more "say": Do we exist as people? Should we?

9

And this is where I leave you: my musings (and I do defer to my Muse), irrespective of form, affirm our light, goodness, humanity in all utterances and ways of being, and reframing Malcolm X a little, here in Harlem, all means being necessary.

A POET'S ESSAY IS A CONVERSATION

Anaïs Duplan

In autumn of 2014, alongside my two friends and collaborators, I wrote customized manifestos for strangers. Every year, at month-long symposiums held in cities around the world, the Utopia School connects people through urgent conversations, performance art, and free workshops with titles like "Intro to Code for People Who Don't Necessarily Like Computers" and "What We Need is Beautiful and Free." The year was 2014 and Utopia School this year was being held at Flux Factory in Long Island City. My friends Danielle Freiman, Kione Kochi and I had come up with a two-day performance called "ManifeStation," where people signed up to fill out a questionnaire and then spend a half an hour with us in our interview booth. We got a variety of people, old and young. We asked folks questions like "What are your hopes? What are your fears?," "Who are you? What are your interests and passions?" and "What do you want this manifesto to accomplish?"

We learned a lot about people in those short interviews. It didn't take long for people to open up. Maybe it was something about the softness of the curtains we'd hung up or the comfort of being at an event like Utopia School, where you know everyone else is weird in the same ways you are. One former physician told us about his difficulties rejecting his parents as an adolescent, about his preoccupation with ancestor worship and his experiences reading R.D. Laing:

"I think of R. D. Laing," he said, "in *The Politics of Experience* where he talks about how children are born—[that] they're innocent, good, and that immediately their parents, schools, etcetera set out to make them feel alienated from themselves, from everything, finally from the earth. If people didn't act this way, we would not even be able to conceive of a nuclear holocaust. I think about the idea that someone thinks they own a plant. I was at this party once, it's outdoors. This flower is withering and it's going to die. But you can't turn the sprinklers on because there's a party going on. Plus the zinnia belongs to the host. I went inside and got some water and watered it. I knew that was considered not right."

After the interviews, Kione and I would get together to talk about the people we'd met and how we might write a manifesto for each of them. We hoped these documents could empower people to pursue the dreams they themselves already held.

In the years after that performance, I began work on *Blackspace*, a book of essays and interviews about the strategies that black and POC writers, artists, and musicians have used, or can use, to work toward psychic and social liberation. I had conversations with poets like Wendy Xu, francine j. harris, Fred Moten, and Nate Mackey. In my conversation with Mackey, I mentioned revisiting his book *Blue Fasa* before our interview and feeling blown away by a quote of Baraka's that Mackey had included in the book's preface. It read: "New Black Music is this: Find the self then kill it." I asked Mackey how we might approach that question as a truly two-part question—part one being to find the black self and part two being to kill it. I include his response here at length:

"That is a statement of Baraka's that I've pondered over for years. One of the things that he meant by that was that, in the course of improvising and getting to the point where you can play free music, you have to find yourself. You have to find out what your sound is. It may be something innate, but you have to practice and find what it is, where it is, and how to get it out, and how to translate it through a horn or a piano or a bass —whatever—which you likely call "technology." How do you technologize yourself? How do you utilize that technology to render something that may be unspeakable, or there before not spoken—and maybe un-renderable? How do you get out a version that at least approximates that self and, at the same time, registers your refusal to be satisfied that you have properly and authoritatively, or with some finality, articulated that self? You have to take that self into the interplay and dialogue and conversation and sometimes, debate and contentious interaction that is involved in playing in an ensemble. In some ways, you have to be prepared to lose that self, or even to be an instrument of losing it, which is to say, to be killing it. That means getting beyond what your prepared repertoire of selfhood is.

"That's some of it but that's not all of it. It's also in the context of a kind of sociopolitical ensembling that was going on at the time that we were involved in. There was tumult among black folks during that period—this is around the mid-sixties— that had come out of the Civil Rights Movement. One of the things that that involved was finding a self— looking at the self that you had and coming to see that it had been fashioned by social relations that we wanted to obliterate. The whole regime of white supremacy and the social mores and instructions and folkways that kept that in place. You had to look at the extent to which you were compliant with that shaping. The self that you had found yourself to be was, in some way, a creation of that regime. Killing it would mean fashioning a new self that would be in conflict with that regime and that wants to bring about the destruction of that regime."

The truth is, freedom is the most mundane thing imaginable, but it's also hard to locate and it's rarely 'pure.' All marginalized people inhabit two worlds at the same time: those of freedom and nonfreedom. Being unfree is different than being in bondage. In bondage, as in the case of enslavement, one's body is owned by someone else. Being unfree, on the other hand, is what happens after the end of enslavement: one becomes an 'emancipated' citizen in the society that used to enslave her and that is still built to do so—without a literal title on one's body, but still with the power to destroy that body, threaten it, circumscribe it, categorize it, and imprison it.

Should we, 'post-bondage,' focus on the ways in which we're free (free to move, free to buy, free to breathe) or the ways we're not-free (free to move but displaced and shuffled around, free to buy but within a capitalist system in which one used to exist as commodity, free to breathe but in especial danger at all times)? I say neither. To locate liberation, one has to locate a third space. This alter-space is not 'outside of,' 'away from' or 'other than' our present world. Instead, it is an intensification, or deepening, of mundane reality.

In a skit that aired during a 2013 episode of *The Eric Andre Show*, the comedian Eric Andre is shown dressed as an NYPD cop, handcuffed to a lamppost with his pants down around his ankles. He begs people from the crowd forming around him to help him pull up his pants. Mocking his masculinity, his authority, Andre makes himself vulnerable to passersby, who look on with a mix of piteous humor and disturbed concern. A black man posing as a failed cop, handcuffed to a phallic post, both assumes the identity of the oppressor and makes a mockery of that oppressor.

The crowd of black witnesses to Andre's prank don't exactly enjoy a moment of catharsis at seeing the disempowered and emasculated policeman. They're trying to figure out whether they should be afraid of Andre (at one point, one man warns the others not to touch him) or if they should help him. The viewers do enjoy the opportunity, however, to intervene in their daily lives with a kind of power otherwise unseen. The temporary release from the mundane provided by the occasion to assist a cop in an embarrassing predicament is also a heightening of the mundane. Andre's vulnerability introduces softness, humanity, and tenderness (as embodied by his nudity) where before—in the masculine, authoritative ideal—there was none. We could describe this performance by Andre as a deliberate misperformance of an archetype of heteronormative masculinity that then frees us from that ideal by exposing it as farcical.

In Aria Dean's video essay for *Dis Magazine*, "Eulogy for a Black Mass," Dean describes the image of blackness as a haunting. "Memes have something black about them," she says. "The something is complicated and hard to make recognizable. It has to do with a lot of black people making memes." On screen, Dean shows memes that show black people dancing, laughing, and enjoying each other's company while her voice describes a pernicious cycle of images of black people circulating around the Internet in a self-referential loop. "Can we bilaterally think blackness through memes and memes through blackness? Both smear, mar, blur ontological integrity," she concludes.

What the video essay as a form reveals to us is the conversational potential of the essay itself. When the essay works as an art object, a poetic object, or as an experiment in video, it is an interview that we come into with an artist. Losing the need to adhere to merely logocentric explication, we come into the possibility of arriving at truth through the integration of thought and sense. The wisdom of the poetic essay is its capacity for aesthetic mystery.

In *Art as Experience*, John Dewey argues that artists use their chosen media as a means to physicalize an internal thinking process. Responding to Keats' idea of negative capability, he writes, "In spite of the elliptical character of Keats' statements two points emerge. One of them is his conviction that 'reasonings' have an origin like that of the movements of a wild creature towards its goal, and they may become spontaneous, 'instinctive,' and when they become instinctive are sensuous and immediate, poetic. The other side of this conviction is his belief that no 'reasoning' as reasoning, that is, as excluding imagination and sense, can reach truth."

Using the tools of computer and social technology, film, and video, black digital media artists like Sondra Perry, Kevin Jerome Everson, American Artist, and Martine Syms have shown us the powerful possibilities of using art to "think through" racism, oppression, and subsequently, liberation. How might we learn from the techniques used by these artists to reconceive of a black avant-garde that uses technology as a language in which to speak about embodiment itself?

Shortly after publishing a collection of poems, *Take This Stallion*, in 2016, I was hungry for another way to express myself. I looked to video as a medium for what I couldn't find in poetry. Poets have a lot of tools for controlling rhythm, cadence, and even speed, but duration in print media is elusive and hard to grasp. In video poetry, I can ask a question and make it last a long time. I can say things really quickly. I can prolong a moment for as long as it needs prolonged.

In conceiving of a 24-hour video poem, *The Lovers are the Audience Who Watch*, I wanted to try to imagine what it would be like to stare into the eyes of a loved one for 24 hours. The video sequence is constructed from found footage — largely taken from music videos and art documentaries on YouTube — where there is a central figure, the artist, who is being watched by an audience, us. I borrowed the title of the piece from a line of poetry by Juliana Huxtable from her collection, *Mucus in My Pineal Gland*. She writes:

> "THE LOVERS ARE THE AUDIENCE WHO WATCH, HYPNOTIZED BY THE SUBLIMITY OF THE PRODUCTION. LAUGHTER IS CUED WHEN ONE OF THE GURLS BLEEDS OR SHITS ON THE OTHER. THE SHOW ENDS WHEN THE TRIFECTA HAVE CONVINCINGLY ORGASMED. THE GURLS STAND IN A ROW, HAVE ALL MAKE-UP REMOVED BY THEIR CORRESPONDING MAN, TAKE A BOW, AND WALK OFF STAGE IN SILENCE.
>
> IS THE CLIT THE ORIGIN AND AM I JUST A SLUT."

Mucus in my Pineal Gland doesn't present itself as a series of cohesive object-ideas (i.e. "poems"), but rather, as a colloquium of voices. For that reason, something feels wrong about calling her book a "poetry collection." Huxtable's poems feel more like Tumblr posts that straddle narrative poetry, speculative fiction, and archival document. They maneuver space, time, and genre. Though there are the occasional moments of lineated verse, Huxtable uses, in her words, a "VISUAL LANGUAGE CASTRATED OF ITS GRAMMATICAL STRUCTURE." The majority of the text is in all-caps, with section titles like "DIVINE BITCHES," made up of prose blocks that extend for pages on end. Huxtable's loose and copious syntax and morphing typographical landscape serve as the engines by which body and text— text and body— become interchangeable with one another.

Like the parts of the body, syntactical grammar relies on a "STRUCTURE WITHIN WHICH ITS MEANING RESIDES." Flesh is the threshold that speaks and that is called upon whenever you refer yourself to me, or I to you. Huxtable maps the body's planes and passageways, while at the same time drafting a map of what it means to make physical contact with someone else, or to hide from that contact. What does it mean to make contact with a poetic speaker? "IT'S PINK INSIDE THE BLACKEST STRETCH / OF FLESHTONE PLANES WHERE GOOSEBUMPS / TAKE PERMANENT RESIDENCE BETWEEN RIDGES / THAT HIDE THE MOON," writes Huxtable in the poem, "MORNING LIGHT ON MY SKIN." With keen awareness of the body's as physical landscape, Huxtable deconstructs the experience of embodiment down into tones, textures, and planes.

For Dewey, the materials that make up art objects themselves aren't meaningful but the way that they converge in a work of art is. The medium in which, or the mechanism by which, materials converge is emotion, a kind of sense-making. Different from the discrete ideas of happiness, sadness, excitement, and anger, emotion here is an amalgamation of qualities. Our senses, our sense organs, provide to us information about the qualities that make up emotion. This information, in tandem with intellectual activity—that is, ideas in language—constitute our entire apparatus for worldbuilding. Truth is made and destroyed by the collective work of these two faculties. If it's true that we can't arrive at truth without the input of the sense organs, then artists, who usually enjoy a keen sensory life, have special tools for learning and researching the external world that non-artists may not have. In particular, black artists have at their disposal these means of self-discovery and a distinct path toward psychic congruence, even in the face of ongoing psychological trauma caused by racism and racist encounters.

For an art praxis to lead to congruence, an artist adopts an all-seeing eye (or all-hearing ear) that lights up the internal world and allows some fact or facet of it to materialize. They carry an insight, but also an external sense that negotiates public and private meaning. This external sense, rather than a burden, is like a kind of proprioception, allowing the artist to know where her body is in space, where her ideas fall in relation to other ideas. Integration happens in degrees. The right work of art—one that settles the large divide between joy and tragedy within me, provides me with an opportunity each time I meet it. What is the experience of psychic coherence? The cessation of thought, a flow state, the opening of the senses to their maximum potential. In experiences of coherence, the meaning of one's existence is self-evident, if inarticulable. Language, an "afterthought," always arises out of some incoherence between self and world, or self and other. Language displaces this incoherence, relocating it to some less troubled site (or sight) of meaning. Like a disease we can finally name, our troubles seem to wane if we can make them, with our words, disappear.

Think of the things you like. What draws you to them? What emotions do you feel in their presence? These are the objects that lie between you and coherence. It's not that desire is bad— quite the opposite. It's that desire is a tool for grasping what remains unincorporated in you. What kinds of conversations do you want to have today? If the media we use are the tools by which we physicalize ourselves, how will you choose to become? By what means? Through which medium? What do you need to say? Can you figure out how to say it to the person who needs to hear it?

BURNING CANE FIELDS

Raquel Salas Rivera

for José Martí

> The vain townsman thinks the whole world is his town, and as long as he gets to be mayor, as long as he mortifies the rival that took his girl, or his savings grow in the piggy bank, all's right with the universal order, having no knowledge of the giants that carry seven tongues in their boots and can push him down with that boot, nor of the comets' celestial war, comets that fly through the sleeping air swallowing worlds. What is left of the town in América must awaken. These days aren't for wearing blinders. These are gun under the pillow days, like Juan de Castellanos soldiers: the weapons of the final judgement, that beat the rest. Trenches forged with ideas are worth more than trenches made of stones.[1]
>
> —José Martí, "Our America"

---

1. My translation. "Cree el aldeano vanidoso que el mundo entero es su aldea, y con tal que él quede de alcalde, o le mortifique al rival que le quitó la novia, o le crezcan en la alcancía los ahorros, ya da por bueno el orden universal, sin saber de los gigantes que llevan siete leguas en las botas y le pueden poner la bota encima, ni de la pelea de los cometas en el cielo, que van por el aire dormido engullendo mundos. Lo que quede de aldea en América ha de despertar. Estos tiempos no son para acostarse con el pañuelo a la cabeza, sino con las armas de almohada, como los varones de Juan de Castellanos: las armas del juicio, que vencen a las otras. Trincheras de ideas valen más que trincheras de piedra."

I.

If I call Martí brother, or even say his brotherhood had no room for me, am I not seeing difference where he saw a putting down of glasses and a raising of weapons? How long is the sentence in an Antillean essay, how long can we draw out our conceits, thinking them only metaphors really, only ways of speaking ourselves into history that may or may not have room? For all the piggy banks and vaults are full of metals, stolen from the Arawaks torn by Juan de Castellano's dogs; and yes, under the pillows are the guns, next to the doors are the bats, on the fridge is the escape plan, within the fascism are the colonies, twisting with the colony is the foil of neo-empire, old stories, sort of, old poems. And the trenches, oh the paper trenches, are either lists of safe houses, or instructions on how to never answer certain knocks, ways of writing ourselves into an "us" forever beyond the scope of this writing.

What does it take to write? Martí wrote by candlelight, in New York, making, as Lola Rodríguez de Tío wrote, Cuba and Puerto Rico, "two wings of the same bird,"[2] because let's be real, this naturalessness was written, this solidarity is not effortless. What then is this moment, when by candlelight Puerto Rico washes clothes with Martí's reused dirty waters, but with different bodies, and breaking over these changes, these differences in century, dying over these differences when most of the island is still without light. How should I read this enlightened antillano, not being us, not being himself, and know it is the poetry, or whatever that means, that gives me some flight and some crash as well.

In his essay on Martí's "Prologue to the 'Niagara Poem' by Juan Antonio Pérez Bonalde,"[3] Julio Ramos argues that Martí's "esthetic [poetical-

---

2. See *Mi libro de Cuba*, pg. 5, Imprenta La Moderna, 1893: "Cuba y Puerto Rico son/ de un pájaro las dos alas,/ reciben flores ó balas/ sobre el mismo corazón…"
3. My translation. See "José Martí Presentación de Julio Ramos: 'Prólogo al 'Poema del

political] drive"[4] exceeds the performance of knowledge enacted by the modern critical exercise. Ramos argues that, in the prologue, Martí "reflects [...] on poetry as the art of the crisis of the subject [and that at the same time] the figurative density of the prologue confirms the esthetic political horizon of a new gaze: a poetic mode of enunciating and of authorizing the discourse about the crisis of experience that drives modernity."[5] This authorization happens through metaphor, and, to borrow from another of Ramos' studies, "in Martí's work, confronts fragmentation and attempts to condense that which has been dispersed."[6] But Ramos also believes he sees in beauty "a conjugating and condensing power" through which future beauty comes into being.[7] Unlike his contemporaries, Martí saw in beauty an alternative set of values that prized things that were not seen as useful, values tied to "'sensibility' that had being impacted by the instrumentalizing logic of capitalism."[8]

And so I meet Martí at the crossroads where he is both hell-bent on paper trenches—when so many Puerto Ricans have no light with which

---

Niágara' de Juan Antonio Pérez Bonalde' (1882)" pgs. 23-29, *Crítica literaria y teoría cultura en América latina*, eds. Clara María Parra Triana and Raúl Rodríguez Freire, Ediciones Universitarias de Valparaíso, 2015.
4. Ibid. "pulsión estética (poética-política)"
5. Ibid. "reflexiona [...] sobre la poesía como un arte de la crisis del sujeto [y que a, su vez,] la densidad figurativa del prólogo confirma el horizonte estético político de una nueva mirada: un modo poético de enunciar y de autorizar el discurso sobre la crisis de la experiencia que acarrea la modernidad."
6. See "'Nuestra América': El arte del buen gobierno," *Desencuentros de la modernidad en América Latina*, pg. 291, Tierra Firme, 2003. "El discurso martiano, nuevamente, se sitúa ante la fragmentación e intenta condensar lo disperso. [...] Su devenir [la historia], en Martí, descompone la totalidad, de cuyo cuerpo originario sólo quedan restos que debían ser rearticulados."
7. My translation. Ibid, pgs (300-301). "En 'Nuestra América, texto armado en torno al poder conjugador y condensador de la metáfora, la literatura se autorrepresenta como el cultivo de esa diseminación, reagrupando las semillas regadas sobre la tierra, y proyectándose como la forma misma del saber del 'árbol'."
8. My translation. See "José Martí Presentación de Julio Ramos: 'Prólogo al 'Poema del Niágara' de Juan Antonio Pérez Bonalde' (1882)" pgs. 23-29, *Crítica literaria y teoría cultura en América latina*, eds. Clara María Parra Triana and Raúl Rodríguez Freire, Ediciones Universitarias de Valparaíso, 2015.

to write, no time or desire—and where he is also so sweet, ready to ask for us to have light, to have the space to love, to desire, to enact beauty. A temporal crossroads, much like writing to the dead, writing to those who cannot read him, a gesture both naïve in its privilege and sincere in its excess, its desire to undo itself through the writing. An act either forever trapped in the narrowest of presents or written for some future reader. A crossroads where he writes as if giving a speech only broken-fisted angels can interpret.

II.

On Sunday, February 11, 2018, an ex-professor wrote to let me know that the administration at the Mayagüez Campus of the University of Puerto Rico was considering putting a moratorium on the Comparative Literature Program. From late September until that evening, I had been helping evacuees come to Philadelphia and had seen, heard, and experienced too much, yet I had somehow kept it together. "Yo he visto el águila herida/ volar al azul sereno,/ y morir en su guarida/ la víbora del veneno. Oculto en mi pecho bravo/ la pena que me lo hiere:/ el hijo de un pueblo esclavo/ vive por él, calla y muere."[9] But this was a new poison, one I hadn't slowly been exposed to. This was the program where I first read "Chip" Delany, Robert Reid-Parr, and Paul Preciado; where I learned about Columbian "nadaista" poets; and where I wrote and performed queer plays with a group of young queer performers. I became a poet there, read theory in a way that allowed me to push against some of the built-in limitations of being an organizer in a colony, where we can only afford so much speculation.

9. See José Martí, Versos Sencillos, pgs. 11-12, Louis Weiss & Co., Impresores, 1891.
"Yo he visto el águila herida/volar al azul sereno,/ y morir en su guarida/ la víbora del veneno.// Oculto en mi pecho bravo/ la pena que me lo hiere:/ el hijo de un pueblo esclavo/ vive por él, calla y muere.// Todo es hermoso y constante,/ todo es música y razón,/ y todo, como el diamante,/ antes que luz es carbón."

I broke down crying.

These were not paper trenches, these were apartments, parks, spaces we opened up, for people we didn't know we'd soon lose. Places where we'd discuss Anjelamaría Dávila, organize the student assembly that approved the strike, and rehearse. This was el Colegio. Many of us had part-time jobs, were working-class and broke, and depended on the Pell Grant. Everything we read was measured against this: what it could offer or detract from our desire to keep living. To believe in things that were deemed useless meant we had to argue for their usefulness on a campus that specialized in engineering and prepared biology students to work for pharmaceutical companies. We had to call our verses paper trenches, even when they weren't, because to call them paper sculptures wouldn't keep out the rain.

I am still bad at this, at advocating for poetry as something that not only I need, but that we need, and it's probably because I'm not sure it's true. We can survive without poetry. It is possible. For too long we've been crafting answers to arguments posed by our enemies. Rather than ask if we can survive without poetry, why not ask why we are always calculating the necessary minimum for survival. What if we marched through the world with military excess, saying I will take a future where there is too much poetry over a present where we constantly have to advocate for our right to dream?

III.

In *Women, Creole Identity, and Intellectual Life in Early Twentieth-Century Puerto Rico*, Magali Roy-Féquière notes that culture nationalism—a nationalist ideology that prioritizes the formation of a national culture and an essentialized "Puerto Ricanness" in lieu of the political independence of the Nation-State—interpellates the Puerto Rican writer to fulfill a contract in which the writer is asked to perform "the awesome task of being a guarantor of the existence of [their] culture." She calls this demand an "enduring ethical dictum" and attributes it with the continuance of a cultural nationalist literary tradition and a parallel counter-discursive tradition that has 'documented' its dominance. The Generación del 30—which consisted of an ex-landowning class of hacendados—after being displaced by U.S. absentee capitalists—offered cultural nationalism as a way of saving Puerto Rican society from political and economic bankruptcy.[10]

In Puerto Rico, poets write essays. We advocate from the poems. We load the forms until they sink to a bottom where silt and time makes them indistinguishable. There is all this writing—poems, essays, history books, novels—writing thrown into the pit of the future, questions phrased as definite statements, as visions, prophecies of paper, not of stone. We have an excess of excess. First, we have a generic proliferation, which is our reiterant response to the failure of the emancipatory cultural nationalist project. If only this time we could say it in just the right way, so our words would legally travel to the mainland and ring in the ears of absentee capitalists. This kind of excess makes it so that we have many essays, poems, stories, and plays that often form part of the same conversation, centered around who we are and how we can finally be free. It also makes it so our poems, stories, and plays often sound like essays.

Then there is the esthetic [poetical-political] drive that exceeds the performance of knowledge enacted by the modern critical exercise. This kind of excess makes our essays sound like poems. Beauty is a democratizing force, a unifying quality that lets us shine through despite and beyond colonialism.

Finally, there is the excess of writing itself. The crossroads where Martí and I intersect and diverge. A suspicious commodity, in the later part of

---

10. See *Magali Roy-Féquière, Women, Creole Identity, and Intellectual Life in Early Twentieth-century Puerto Rico*, pg. 4, Temple University Press, 2004. "To counter the all-encompassing sense of social and cultural dislocation, the intelligentsia proposed to discover anew Puerto Rico's 'national character' in order to affirm the existence of the nation and to provide the discourses that would buttress new political projects."

the twentieth century, Puerto Rican poets went from being champions of a cultural nationalist project to unnecessary expenditures. This kind of excess makes the writing feel all the more urgent. True, the fight against the privatization of beaches and the fight against the elimination of a Comparative Literature Program are separate and the impulse to compare them is rooted in class and racial differences, but after the PROMESA bill was passed, neoliberal efforts that had been fragmented were consolidated. In the span of a few months, the minimum wage and the university budget were both slashed, though with varying effects. The Puerto Rican bourgeoisie, under the auspices of U.S. imperial interests, has long insisted that we sacrifice for an imagined community, with a very unimagined leadership.

It takes a certain amount of privilege to believe education is a privilege, even if you are using that idea to argue that it shouldn't be, for although much of our knowledge has been privatized through institutions, in Puerto Rico, those universities have often played a radicalizing role. Literature, history, and philosophy classrooms have been where many young working-class Puerto Ricans first felt permission to explore possibilities beyond survival, beyond the bare bones of stripped-down trees, ravaged by the hurricane of unending poverty and colonial oppression.

Rather than argue that literature is a necessary excess, I'd like to embrace excess on its own terms. We are already excessive, supplemental, and contingent. We have been made non-consensually dependent. We are way too much all the time and everywhere. Cultural nationalism bifurcates forms in an attempt to hold back a scream, to colonize a desire to burn down cane fields, but this attempt is more often than not unsuccessful. In her essay, "On the Perilous Potential of Feminist Silence," Carina del Valle Schorske writes:

> [In] Puerto Rico this summer, my voice melted into the melodic din—but its edge sharpens against the performance of white silence. Which is not, in fact, silent: it's a careful repertoire of subdued gestures, coded words, and background expectations about who should speak, when, how, and how much. The unconscious

expectation is that words coming from white people—especially white men—are not an interruption, but part of the "white noise" of our social world. The background track. Latina expressivity is not just a value-neutral cultural norm that appears exaggerated in relation to the different cultural norm of white restraint. It shows up as a form of resistance to the fact that the white valorization of silence—or, at the very least, "appropriate" affect—always seems strictest when it comes to us.[11]

Whiteness, like Frederic Jameson's description of the Bonaventure, allows the interlocutor to see without being seen and projects a certain aggressiveness towards and power over an Other. It is flat, smooth, digestible, and ductile. The white body is an easy body that purges its bitterness inward. Puerto Ricans come already marked. We are bad citizens, bad fathers, bad mothers, bad children, bad lovers, bad americanos. We perform being los más mejores in order to receive prizes and speak in essays, adding our good days to the elegy's archive. We are asked to verify our bodies, our voices, and check for the curvature, the greña, the murusa. We are expected to have buenos modales that aim to get rid of malas mañas, a las buenas o a las malas. Bad writing only exists as something signaled, something determined by another, imposed text. Las malas palabras rise to the surface with rage, with the tempest, with the tapón, when we hit the bureaucratic wall, when our house floods, when the plumber doesn't arrive and there isn't light in the whole neighborhood. The malas palabras are cafre.

What if we refuse the imperative to write ourselves into colonial methodological traditions? Let's do it. Let's be cafres in the essays and the poems and keep writing too many. Let's dwell on these failed and excessive moments when "the awesome task of being a guarantor of the existence of [our] culture" is saturated by the "esthetic [poetical-political] drive," the moments when we get too hype. Let's hold on tightly to the

---

11. See Carina del Valle Schorske, "Feminist Silence: Clarice Lispector, Alejandra Pizarnik, and Poetic Voice(lessness)," Literary Hub, https://lithub.com/on-the-perilous-potential-of-feminist-silence/, November 1, 2016.

belief that we have a right, not just to survive, but to live excessively, to reclaim that excess that has been stolen. We want it back. And what if we release our daily grief, even for a few hours and allowed ourselves all the rage and all the future bliss we've been containing, what would that look like? How impossibly fucking beautiful would that be?

FOUR SHORT AND UNFINISHED ESSAYS (WITH POEMS) FROM THE RUINS OF JAPANESE AMERICAN INCARCERATION

Brandon Shimoda

as part of Contradictions, The Sea, and The Snow: A Poem-Essay as the Open Space, featuring Myung Mi Kim and Cecilia Vicuña (March 3, 2018)

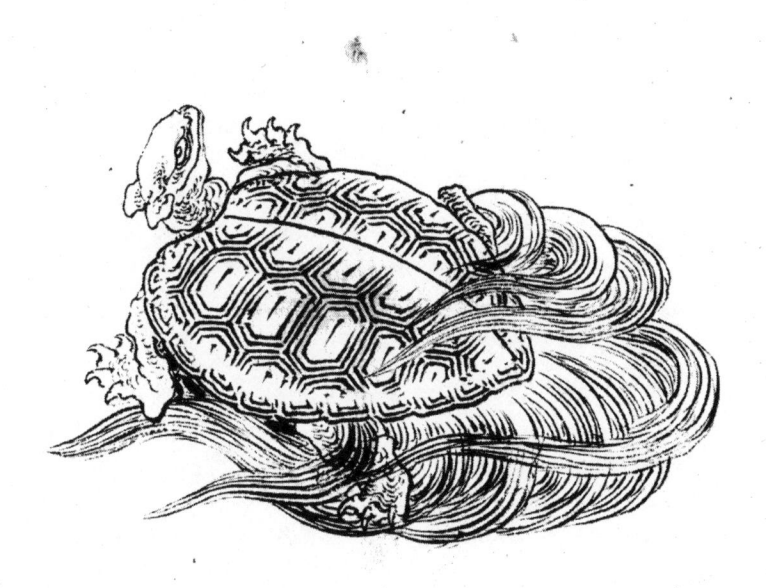

Katsushika Hokusai (1760–1849)

This year marks the thirtieth anniversary of the signing of the Civil Liberties Act (August 10, 1988), the federal law with which the United States closed the book on the mass incarceration of Japanese immigrants and Japanese American citizens during World War II. I begin here because any attempt at writing or talking about writing—in poetry, essays, et cetera—begins in the place I cannot (or cannot seem to) escape, the place with which writing has become inseparable if not synonymous. I say begin, but I mean re-enter, although re-enter is also not right. One of the immigrants who was incarcerated was my grandfather, who is dead. One of the citizens who was incarcerated was my great-uncle, who is also dead. Another one of the citizens was my cousin, who is alive, and has said very little about it. Another one of the citizens was another one of my cousins, who is also alive, and who has also said very little about it. Another one of the citizens was my great-aunt, who is also alive, and does have things to say about it, but only recently started saying things about it, including to her children, who are in their forties, and did not, until recently, know very much, if anything, about their mother's three and a half years as an enemy of the United States. Actually, the United States did not close the book; it took a razor blade, cut out every word, and rearranged each one, in dreadfully predictable configurations, across the pages of twenty-first-century American existence. What happened on August 10, 1988? Some of my relatives, living and dead, might say that what happened on August 10, 1988 was that they were redeemed for an injustice committed against them. But the Civil Liberties Act was not an act of reconciliation. It was an act of control. It galvanized, out of voluminous testimony and traumatization, a regeneration of silence.

I am, as far back as I can trace, the only poet in my family. I share that solitude with the altar. The altar is where my ancestors continue their attempts to materialize a picture of the future that might justify what they were made or compelled to endure, while recognizing that their endurance will not deliver them to the realization of that picture, nor will the future be as auspicious or endurable as they imagine. Poetry is, for me, the placing of an orange on the altar. I know the orange will sit there, slowly expiring beneath its skin. But I also have faith it will be touched, that my ancestors will be nourished.

On the occasion of the thirtieth anniversary of the Civil Liberties Act, then, I would like to share four short and unfinished essays from the ruins of incarceration. Essays, and also rehearsals. If poetry is the placing of the orange on an altar, essays are the cleaning of the altar, in preparation for the orange. The first three take place in the Gila River concentration camp on the Gila River reservation near where I live in Arizona, and the last one takes place in bed. I hope they express some part of an answer to the question our presence today is asking.

•••

Don't get too close to the ditches, the older boys said. *If you do, the snapping turtles will grab you and pull you in.* The young girl did not see any ditches. It was her first day in the desert. She was six. The desert was flat. Except for a few hills that looked like they were hiding something. Over the next three and a half years, the young girl would grow familiar with and knowledgeable about and even in love with the desert, if love is not too strange to say, or even feel. She was in the desert because she was put there. By her country, the United States. Which looked at her, or did not look at her, and determined that she was their enemy. Which meant also, because she was an American citizen, that she was her own enemy, but what did that mean? What are snapping turtles? What happens when they grab you? What happens when they pull you in? She thought of hundreds, thousands, of snapping turtles, waiting at the bottoms of the ditches, with yellow eyes like squash and green eyes like zucchini, to grab her and pull her in. That is how you become a snapping turtle, she thought, that is how you stop being a human and become a snapping turtle. But how do you become an enemy? Maybe love is what you call the feeling you gain from being familiar with and knowledgeable about a person or place, desert or ditch, with which you are forced to be in relation, indefinitely. The young girl looked at the desert, the hills that looked like they were hiding something, then at the barbed wire, and, looming above the barbed wire, the guard tower, on which was standing a potato-faced man, who was partly obscured by the gun that was aimed at her face. She thought of a cross, and a man, several men, hanging upside-down, their heads almost touching the shadow of their heads on the ground. Over the next three and a half years, guns would be ever present and, as far as the young girl knew, always loaded. The guns, however, were not as terrifying as the potato-faced men who held them.

•••

When the children arrived, there were turtles Snapping turtles
like helmets greeted the children
Turtles deep
deep deep in the ditches, slowly rose   and snapped at the children
like Yoshiko, wearing a dress   of her mother' s crumpled face,
walked right up to the ditch
and peered in: children were grabbed, pulled in, became turtles
Their eyes were olives. Children were torches

•••

In the ruins of the third largest of the concentration camps in which Japanese Americans were incarcerated, is a field of cotton that, when seen from the hill overlooking the ruins, resembles a field of snow. The resemblance of snow adds an air of refreshment to the desert. Arizona cotton is exceptionally white. Agronomists say it is because it never rains in the desert, rain is dirty, but who can look at a field of cotton without seeing desecrated bones? Gila River is the reservation of the Pima and Maricopa people. It was occupied from July 1942 to November 1945 by the United States Army, in the form of a concentration camp, in which 13,348 Japanese immigrants and Japanese American citizens were incarcerated, making it, between those years, the fourth largest city in Arizona. It is the only incarceration site that requires permission to enter. The tribal council is protective of their land, crowded as it is on all sides by the ravages of unsacred living. Gila River, the *river*, stopped running a century ago. Occasionally, when it rains many days in a row, the river returns, only to disappear just as quickly. During the war, cotton farmers begged the government to release Japanese Americans from Gila River. *We need them to pick our cotton*, the white farmers begged. One hundred volunteered. *We need more of them to pick our cotton*, the white farmers begged again. No more volunteered. The farmers became angry, complained that the Japanese Americans were lazy, that life in the camps was too easy. Ditches are easy. Snapping turtles are easy. To locate one's fear in what cannot be seen is too easy. Eleanor Roosevelt arrived. She looked out at the 13,348 and said, beneath her smile: *I would try very hard not to have too many of them in the same place.* Then, to feign that she and *them* were being nourished by the same source of giving, she raised a glass of milk to her lips, took a sip, winced, and pronounced the milk: *sour*. Depending on the season, the field of cotton resembling a field of snow might also resemble: desecrated bones; the sky reflected in a flooded grave; or sour milk.

•••

Eleanor shook herself off

Japanese Americans were not looking at themselves
turning white not the cotton not the descendants of bloodless cotton
the children's fathers refused
to pick children were shy had stories to tell,
not their own, but those not resolved, still dirty

•••

a nisei woman was asked if she would like to speak, to share her story
the people
facing the gleaming snow
looked sad, for a moment, then vulturous. sad again
expectant, ready to ascend. The nisei woman shook her head, No, she said.
Are you sure, she was asked. I don't remember enough to share She said
As she was looking through the snow She remembered everything
but could not, seven decades later, associate herself with the subjects,
by whom her memory was reminded. They too were painted
white effigies

∴

We used to dig holes beneath the barracks to stay cool, the young girl said. *We cut holes in the floors, and built sunken rooms.* The metaphors of being forced underground, into hiding, and being forced to dig one's own grave, came to mind, and I wondered if these metaphors came to the minds of the people as they sat in the holes. The young girl is now eighty-two years old. Her name is Yoshiko, which, depending on the character, means Virtuous Child, Fragrant Child, Grateful Child. I stood with her in a reconstructed barracks in a museum in San Jose. She was my tour guide. *Is this what it felt like?* I asked. *This is what it felt like*, she said, then said: *this is what it feels like*, which I took to mean that living in a concentration camp felt like being part of an exhibition, and despite that, that there were no metaphors. The people of Portland, Los Angeles, rural Arkansas, made Sundays out of gathering on the outside of the barbed-wire fences to watch the Japanese Americans. They brought sandwiches, lemonade. They were like Dante and Virgil, poets overseeing, but ultimately untouched by, the inferno. The exhibition was not, however, limited to the Sunday people, but everyone in the United States, many of whom, whether they felt vindicated or elated or infuriated or resigned or indifferent, to the fate of the Japanese Americans, took one look through the fence and immediately forgot what they were looking at.

∴

You don't forget You are tricked,
  into putting your hand in   mirror-green water. Your hand stays stuck

The snow goes unpicked the motions of refusal compromised
 by our willingness to open the earth of its recollection

only children remember to forget with such warm innocence
It resembles being struck by the sun
not innocence Guilt is not the opposite of innocence
But like the dissolution of a flower into a fruit, compensation

The prisoners cut rectangles in the floor   The guards lent saws

The prisoners dug holes in the dirt
The prisoners fell asleep in the holes
The prisoners disintegrated Not even their secrets

•••

I slept for one year with a photograph of my grandfather. Under my pillow, sometimes under my body. I wanted to sink with him through the bed, through the floor, into the ground, to commingle with what of him had been arrested. The photograph was taken in the Department of Justice prison where my grandfather was incarcerated under suspicion of being a spy for Japan. He was a photographer, more importantly an immigrant, which made him guilty in the minds of his accusers. The first time I saw the photograph it was hanging on the wall of the museum where the prison once stood. In the photograph, my grandfather is wearing a bra and a slip. His hair is standing straight up off his head. And he is smiling. In her book, *Moving Images: Photography and the Japanese American Incarceration*, Jasmine Alinder writes: *It is photographs of Japanese American incarceration that naturalize the state of exception with the false assurance of a smile.*

This is what happened at night: my grandfather slipped out of bed. I woke to see him mounting the wall. I watched him rise up the wall and curve onto the ceiling. I watched him slide down the wall and curve onto the floor. The moment my grandfather touched the floor, two voices emerged: the voice of a young woman and the voice of an old man. The voices emerged behind my right ear, as if out of my shoulder. Their voices were clear—I could hear every word—and materialized, with their voices, a room beneath my room. I wondered if the young woman (she-who-invites) and the old man (he-who-invites) were related. I had the feeling they were the same person, in two different phases of being: the young woman at the furthest limit of herself as an immigrant before becoming a citizen, the old man at the furthest limit of himself as a citizen before becoming a corpse. I tried, every night, to write down what they were saying, but their voices became softer, blurred together, and I realized I never got further than cleaning.

The orange is recursive. Poetry is not what I write, but what I remember of what I have written. The transcription of these voices and the ultimate impossibility of transcribing these voices has become my attempt at writing poetry as well as my attempt to release myself from the attempt at writing poetry.

Note: Parts of this essay were previously published in *The Desert* (The Song Cave, 2018) and *The Grave on the Wall* (City Lights, 2019).

THE POET'S ESSAY *Cecilia Vicuña (transcription)*

Vicuña breathes three times into the microphone.

First,
I would like you to look at the clouds.
See how they are moving

She turns to look at the clouds through the windows behind her, pauses for a moment, then turns back around to face the audience.

ever so slowly.

Think of what just happened.
And it's probably still happening near us—
a fassssst wind
the oooocean maaaking a fast, raging wind.

I learned a new word:
bombogenesis—
giiiiiving birth to a bommmmb cyclone
a boooomb that raaapidly intensifies
a stooorm that coinciiides with the fuuull moon.

I wanted to respond
to essay an essay,
but I realized
that you can't essay an essay in English.
you can 'ensayar' in Spanish
you can 'essayer' in French.
but you CAN'T
not c – u – n – t
but c – a – n – t
you can't essay in English.

Why is that constant
borrowing of Latin
stopping at the moment
of making the word
essay itself?

I wanted to avoid
or it wanted to avoid
the weight
too much
is madness
of essaying
with itself.

The essaying doing an essay,
but what does it say the eeeeeee
and the ehhhSAY?

ehhh concha tu madre. Despierta, HEH!
Despieeeeerta, eh.
In truth, it is the 'e,'
the energy
the eeehhhnergy in the eeehhhssence part of the word ehhhssay
the eehhssence rooted out

by the military police of academia.

Ehhhhssence. They say: *shut up,
don't ever sayyy that word.*

But the ehhh in ehhhssence says:
*SPEAK UP. E – SSAY
say say say.*

What lives inside the ehhhssay in the ehhhssay?

I wonder, what is it about the poet's essay that gathers us here,
that calls you to invite us to think and write about that?

In truth, I share what Raquel Salas said before,
is she around here?
Ah! Muy bien, tu boca roja.

Raquel said that in Latin America the poet's essay is something else—so else so else so else—that you could even hardly think that it is an essay, because practically every poet has to do a poet's essay. And this essay starts so full of quick-wittity madness and beauty and rocks and smells that the last thing you are thinking is that they are an academic essay.

So, all this desire that was in your invitation to liberate us from the oppression of the thesis didn't affect the Latin American poets. And that's what bred the woman, the person, that I am. To answer to your hidden question inside the question about what in the poem is different from an essay, I remembered the girl reading those essays, and I think that what drew me to them is that I could see, feel, the thoughts and the shape of the unfolding structure of the thoughts more clearly in those Latin esses – Esses? Essays – than perhaps in the poem itself. As if the essay had a will, a desire to show itself—to transparent its doing while the poem does not. The poem is like us*—full of dirty things, full of dirt and dark parts within. The poem is happy to hide its doing and show only un destello, un vislumbre—a sighting of the mystery involved in its being.

If the poem is the creature, an organism, an autonomous construct, a place where we pick or perceive structures beyond our knowing, our naming, our *barruntar* as we say in Spanish, which is to sense what cannot be really sensed, the essay instead may be a field, a playground to observe the limits and boundaries, the shapes of our thoughts.

If the poem is phenomena, perhaps the essay is what is now called the epiphenomena. And that may be the power of the poet's essay, as the border, the meeting place for opposite life forms, cleaves by the clashing experience of its not being exactly what it's supposed to be.

When your invitation first came, I wrote it this way:

It said: ehhssay… the ehhnergy of the saying, looking at itself. And last night, as I was thinking: *what on earth am I doing here?* I drew this baby. Of course, you can't see.

That's perhaps the point.

It's a self-portrait. Me, naked. There is an *E* that she is holding on the right hand and there is a *SAY* she is holding on the left. The left is the speaker. And in the middle coming up all the way from underneath, I said *their* like some ladies here or some men too. They're *their* person. That's a beautiful thing.

So, their – or her as you wish – snake of the *S* is coming around and coming and taking the place of her voice, her red thread snake voice.

And when I drew that I thought, *you will not feel that the same way I do*, because perhaps you see, I am a colonized, a doubly colonized, Indian. I was colonized first by Spanish and then colonized by English, so I can take no more.

Even as a child, my mother, who was a Spanish-speaker Indian, she would say to me: *Why do you speak like that? Like if you were eating the words?*

Maybe I was cannibalizing them.

And so, from the very beginning, I saw words in a weird way. And so here, there's another drawing of the naked woman. You see where she thinks she's naked? That's how I used to write when I was not in a cold, cold place as here. Write naked. So, there she is holding the *W* of *weaving* on the right hand and on the left she's holding the *ORDS* of the *words*. Do you know what that *ord* really means? *Ord* is an ancient root that makes the word *order*, that makes the word *warp*, that makes the word *art*.

All of it began by the weaving or dealing* in the warp of the ancient weaver-thinkers that created these colonial languages that we use now, because no matter how colonized or colonizer a language can be, stiiiill it holds the memory of those ancient weavers that created those concepts and names.

Since we were meant to speak about the ocean,
I don't know how much more time we have,
because I can't keep track of time.
But I don't want to bore you
because I'm looking forward to talking with you.
And so, I will stop anytime,
but I will go on for a little while.

So, I said, my essay began in Concón. My life as an essay, as a conscious essay, began in Concón. And here I realize that I'm reading your invitation wrong when you sent out this phrase:
a poem-essay as the open space. I immediately turned it into: *a poem-essay* IN *the open space,* because that was my rebellion as a child. I did not believe that writing was writing as it was being taught to us in school. I began writing with acts. I began writing by the sea and with the sea. I

wrote, *to resist is to exist because exist is inside resist.*

Now the place where that occurred is called Connnncón. There's no memory of the ancient indigenous language that called that place Connnncón, but there are traces of a language so old that it may have been spoken by the first inhabitants of this place in the Pacific Ocean in the middle of Chile at the foot of the Aconcagua Mountain.

If that was the case, the meaning that has remained is that CON means the life-force of the ocean. The life force. And the circulation from ooocean to raaain to clouuud to snooow to river to oceannnn. So CON is not just the water or the ocean or the life force, but it is the entire circular process, the entire movement of one turning into the other. And in the indigenous language of Chile when you want to intensify a meaning, you double it. You intensify by saying Connnnncón, which means *life force, life force*. Think of the Western ways where to intensify is to speed up to a killer degree.

But seen from the Spanish, *con* is the root of consciousness, the root of together, so you are in Connnncón, you are with the sea. You are with the awareness of the ocean itself.

I have just done a book about my relationship with that *con*. It is called *About to Happen*. But I am not doing to – *doing* I said, I'm not *doing* instead of *going*. It's much better *doing* than *going*. I'm not *going* to speak about that.

I will now go back to the essay word. They are saying a way of writing in the lannnnndddd andddddd of the land. This is because I just returned from Tierra del Fuego, The Land's End. And over there I'm working with a group that calls itself Ensayos.

Calls it-sell, I said.
They are selling themselves.
I am part of that.

YES
we are saying that we are ensaaaayos.
So what is the ensayo? Is it the writing or the being?
Or the being there? In Tierra del Fuego?
We can speak about that later.

The ehhhsay.
We are essays of this earth.
Human comes from guman
Not woman like woman: W – O
but G – U – A
G – U – M – A – N
guman, which means 'of the earth.'
She is essaying a form of consciousness in us,
but we have failed so far to read the energy of the saying.
We know how to *breathe* but not how to *BE* in her presence.
Not how to *be* in relation to others and the laaaaand.
Instead of that we have created machines to think in our place.

You probably know, as I do, that these machines we created are already creating algorithms that humans can't read. And they are already changing the world to fit their needs and not ours. So, this idea of the anthropocene, it may end faster than it's beginning thanks to this AI.

And that is how I'm going to slowly wind down, and I'm going to skip, as I usually do, half the notes.

La Mar Oceana, we say in Spanish. The indigenous people forced to speak in Spanish never adopted that notion that the ocean could be male. And they say la marrrrr, la muerte del mar.

The fisherman still call her SHEEE.

And my love is writing a long piece about Nammu*2. This is the name the ocean received at the first time of writing, in Mesopotamia, probably five-thousand years ago. And this is the piece by him. It says: *Our cosmic mother Nammu is depicted in the Mesopotamian clay tablets as the primeval ocean from which everything comes forth.*

Yet, when the actual writing that has come to us in the *Enuma Elish*, written probably between the third and the second millenia BC,

she has already been replaced **singing**
by Tiamat
and Tiamat is then murdered
by her own offspring Marduk,
The male sky god.
After that, Nammu
is never heard from again.
The ocean mother of heaven
on earth was split—

torn apart
by her son
and her body parts
scattered to
all corners of
the earth.

                    James O'Hern

Think of our killing the ocean now,
and you will see we're still in the male logic,
the colonizing, imperial logic.

that logic
that logic
killing

the ocean
mother

Gracias.

*1 You ymmm me kimmm so beautiful name.
*2 Nammu:
In Sumerian mythology Nammu was the Goddess sea (Engur)(…)
the source of life-giving water and fertility in a country with almost
no rainfall.(…) Reay Tannahill in *Sex in History* (1980) singled out
Nammu as the "only female prime mover" in the cosmogonic myths of
antiquity.
https://en.wikipedia.org/wiki/Nammu

RECESS AND NONSENSE   *Fred Moten*

1.

In "Whiteness as Property," Cheryl Harris produces an analysis of whiteness as *a* property, as a mode of property, as something that can be owned and traded and placed in exchange to the advantage of the one who owns it. In so doing, she allows and requires us to think of whiteness not only as a mode of property but also as the very principle, or the very essence, of property. Let's say, but only for the briefest of unaccompanied moments, that if whiteness *is* property, then blackness is the active and ani*mater*ial sufferance of impropriety. More + less than either property's objection or abjection or mere opposition, blackness is the critique of property, on the one hand, and the celebration of dispossession, on the other. This other hand means the critique is anticipatory: that it is not only before what it critiques but that it brings what it critiques into something almost like existence; in turn, what Karen Barad might call the intra-active bothandedness of anticipation instantiates celebration not only as enjoyment but also as solemnity *en masse*. Saidiya Hartman teaches us about a certain heartlessness—given in and as the brutality of the concept of property's belated, reactionary, regulatory power—whose debilitating anesthetics of grasp is, in turn, the most fundamental of the properties of the concept, as such. There has been no more terrible burden, whose imposition we depose beforehand, and no more terrible beauty, whose appositions we turn in restlessly preformative shift, than being-enjoined to celebrate dispossession. When possession is the motivation and constitution not only of the world, but of the very idea of world, earthly existence must bear a homelessness that no person, if the theory of personhood is to be believed, can bear; in this regard, neither hoping, or even fighting, for a place in this world nor any gesture or movement toward the otherworldly will do. This is all to say that to say that whiteness is the principle of property is to say that the modality in which whiteness can "live" or the modality in which whiteness is *endured* or *survived*, is *spatial*. But this, in turn, is to say that whiteness isn't just a venal, brutal, vicious way of taking up space. Whiteness is, rather, the way in which so-called subjectivity is constituted as spatial or, more precisely, as spatiotemporal coordination, so that whiteness in its spatiality is also manifest (immediately, as it were) as a brutal way of taking up, or taking other people's, time. But to be a subject, to be a person, to be white, isn't just to take up space-time in a fucked-up way. What's at stake, rather, is that confluence—that meaningful but contentless placement or emplotment—where whiteness, subjectivity and a bloodlessly and bloodily abstract spatiotemporality converge, constitute one another and are given, in that mutual constitution, as being-in-the-world. One special way to describe that confluence—special because it is a deep intensification of the exaltation and shame that goes with it—is being a poet, which is to say being a citizen of the world of poetry. Whatever it has been to settle for such necessarily colonial settlement, wherein the poet can be said to (dis)own the air and dirt and flesh he does not love, blackness—in its inveterate earth(l)iness—is more + less than that, too.

2.

I guess you could say that if whiteness is the transcendental aesthetic, then blackness is aesthetic immanence and imminence. But this, too, is too stark to remain uncut. Blackness isn't a pole; it's an impure refusal of bipolarity. And Nathaniel Mackey says we're *angels of dust*, after all, so we can't forget the asymmetries of sovereignty, its Apollonian isolation, its sociopathic singularity, the optic whiteness of its whiteness, its tendency to be or go rogue. States don't have a right to exist. Do peoples? Do people? Do persons have such a right? Do poets? Perhaps existence obliterates the economy of rights. Can persons be self-determining? Are atoms self-determining? Does the kind of determinism that Einstein and Bohm desire imply something on the order of a more broadly physical self-determination of/in nature? Are these two kinds of determination cognate? These are questions of black study, given in the open idiom of black poetry. What is revealed in their iteration is that there is no ontological, aesthetic, political, metaphysical, or physical fundament whose rest black study does not disturb.

3.

When J. Kameron Carter asks, "what are the god terms that underwrite human/political/aesthetic sovereignty?" isn't he asking us to ask after how man not only sets but is those terms? Why did man become God? What protocols of cold overrepresentation serially reproduce this collective psychosis which, for fun, in slapstick echo of Carter's elegant echo of Sylvia Wynter, you could call Anselm's mirror stage? (Anselm the Saint, I mean, not saintly Anselm the Berrigan.) What if the first step is the assumption of a body? What is it, Gayle Salamon, to assume a body? To take up a body? To take onto oneself a body? For the body and the self to take one another on in an all but hopelessly soulless dance? What remains beyond that address? What if that address, that aggressively impossible refusal of vulnerability, that projective settlement, is sovereignty, man? And what if the taking up or on of whiteness is, as it were, a step within that step that is continually reactivated when property imposes and supervises the giving and taking of properties and names? Meanwhile riot, muck, mutiny, the general strike, the remorseless working, the undercommon tragicomedy, its antinomian swerve and quarrel, living's dissolute spread, its dispersive largesse, its transubstantial fade, seem always already to have been a black thing you wouldn't understand because it passeth understanding and it ain't no thing. Can we speak, then, and superpositionally, to some insubstantial pageantry of the phonically anasubstantial? Can we make, and share, much ado about black women's rioting (I mean writing, "in rough ranks, in seas, in windsweep")? Are substance and sovereignty so bound up with one another (substance being the real physical matter, that which has mass, occupies space, is on time['s line]) that we have to imagine something like an unreal, or, more properly, surreal physical matter so we can get the body, which is to say the man, off of our b(l)ack and out of our eye? These are question for Gwendolyn Brooks and Alice Walker, which Brooks and Walker teach us how to ask. Meanwhile, Octavia Butler, Toni Morrison, and Hortense Spillers—in some enchanted 1987—teach us that flesh *is* surreal physical matter, which neither has nor occupies. So that what's at stake is the necessity of flesh's more emphatic exhabitation, as something other than withdrawn or withheld or reduced body, as that which is, therefore, apposed to body, to the aesthetics or poetics of self that is the body's assumption and vampiric animation, man. They hate our flesh and want to destroy it and its memory. That genocidal duress is given in a theft of body that follows the body's brutal imposition, a dual operation whose duration is the crack of a whip or the report of a gun or the whisper or the oath of a rapine proposition. But oh, for a poetics of flesh! Oh, for a poetics of selflessness! One wants to speak (of) (through) (as) flesh in its own terms; but flesh has no terms and one can't speak. And yet, we love it for what it gives. Having no mass, flesh is the critical celebration of (the) mass. Flesh is displacement—transformational, gravitational warp. Flesh is the nonsense of the irreducibly (con)sensual. Flesh is descent in anagential consent. Flesh is the cœnobitic jam. Flesh is recess. That's what she says and she says, says Akilah Oliver.

4.

What if "death"—which is the neutral term given here for the loss of some one of us that is inflicted upon that one and some other/s of us by some one/s or other/s of us within and by way of the institutional determination that the one who is lost is not worth keeping—isn't quite the right word for that to which we respond? What if "death" is a calculated reduction of the genocidal, geocidal brutalities we survive? What if what "death" misnames is a brutal response to our survival? These questions concern the terror of counting, of being counted, of being accounted for and accountable in a moral and political and libidinal economy that is utterly committed to the vicious conversion of sharing into ownership, which is the omnicidal regulation of life, its submission to a vicious equilibrium. In this regard, individuation is the fruit and the guardian of that commitment and "death" is individuation's self-management. If, on the other hand, you don't believe in any body, and you don't believe in any thing, then "death" fades into degeneration's regenerative work and play, which makes a different kind of problem for thinking when the ruse of "death," given in and as the materiality of murder, is man-made, massive, naturalized, sanctioned by capital and induced by and in and under the protection of the state. Geocide and genocide, then, not individual calculation; a general rather than a restricted economy, which the collection of the "deaths" of single beings—and all the mattering and not mattering of single (black) lives—hides in (self-)righteous nomination and enumeration. The interplay of individuation and "death" obscures the complexity and shared incompleteness of what is lost. It obscures rather than highlights the specific—which is to say open and striated sets of—differences, which don't just remain but proliferate, past the inadequate metaphysics of the lost and kept, or the lost and found. The open set of differences that I call my mama, or my mama's or my mamas, survive them in dispersion and disbursal. My grandfather planted trees. I'm still (not) my (grand)mama's baby. They were all killed by the same machine that is killing me and my children and insofar as that is true even in the midst of their regenerate survival, the word "death" does them a double wrong by whitewashing their absence and erasing their presence. But what if the death of one who is said to have an individual life only upon their demise, which they must somehow claim and own as well, is a trick of the carceral, governmental, political picturing, and construction of a cryptal funnyhouse? What if individual lives and deaths, contorted in a constant economy of collection and division, are conceptual dematerializations, abstractions used to control and obscure possessed, possessive assault—when *Phantasie* and *le réel* disappear in one another—in and on entangled social life, which is given in finitude's shared endlessness? What if the regulatory calculation, which is of necessity the miscalculation, of transformation is elemental to racial-sexual capitalism's ge(n)ocide machine? What if the brutal imposition of contingency, along the racial and sexual lines that subdivide the sensing differential in the name of (The) Man, is tantamount to the monetization of (how we ornament) disorder? What if "death"—as conceptual tool and real abstraction—is how debt's entropy is held and stolen in a credit economy? The venal, viral mathematics of "death" is already given in the terrible distribution of one life at a time. To just generally disbelieve in any thing and any body is to sense the incalculable, the un(ac)countable, the sexy, the nasty, the no-count, unvalued, attractive, intractive, existential mess of wealth and needs that bosses and owners constantly submit to civil butchery. The Man—in his endless sending of his capitalized, militarized replicant, The Drone—will kill every one of us because He can't kill us all. It is not well for Him to know that more than we do, when another sacrament is at hand, on a hand other than the politico-ecclesiastical performativity of ingestion. What did Anselm mean by debt? Here's where moratorium comes into play: a recess, a postponement, a refusal to settle accounts, instantiates an already given sociality, a blurring—Mackey might whatsay creaking—of the word, given in and as the disavowal of ends when the unpayable, the unsettleable, is announced as radical disruption of the very idea of accounting, of accountability, of the account. Debt and "death" ring out in the horn's populated air, bare silence come back in breathy thicknesses to tell us that assuming a body is like exhuming a body, or ingesting a body, only bloodier. You can't take this. This is not my body. Nobody here. Not here. In this displacement, we flesh. Love that.

5.

This is for an analytic of radical dissatisfaction, of the generally and radically unsatisfactory. I know why we're justified in claiming home/self/body, but the justification doesn't make it right and what we claim ain't good just because we claim it. A state's existence isn't a function of right or rights; its existence is a function of might which then appeals to a logic of right/s, of justification embedded in the brutalization it extends in attempting to negate it. But that state's justification doesn't translate into its right to exist. If there were a right to exist, wouldn't it be predicated on what you've done rather than any possible argument regarding what or why you are, as if these were separable from what and how you do? And yet what could any sovereign entity ever do to justify its existence? This is not a philosophical question about what might happen; this is an underphilosophical question about what has happened. How do we come to accept what we already know about the already existing and about what we need? How do we consent to what we are and what we need rather than constantly and brutally and impossibly assert what we are in the taking of what we want?

6.

I love black people too much to be around them at school. I want to be where we are everywhere. I love black people in an absolutely anabiological way. I don't care about the black community. That's an antisocial artifact of exclusion for which I have neither nostalgia nor desire. The black community is the racial capitalization of what Laura Harris calls "the aesthetic sociality of blackness." I just want to go home. If I say this here it's only because I can't say it at school, where we chant appropriation in public by ourselves, for reasons of diversity and inclusion. I'm only here right now if you think I am, or if you think you are. Who all here will have allowed (for) that? But, you know, to yield to the attraction of a specific analysis that comes out of a series of interlocking exclusions but is irreducible to those exclusions and is, rather, given and instantiated in a set of erotic practices would mean not only to acknowledge an already given and constantly regenerated and regenerative blackness but also to take up an open set of specific designs on engaging in those erotic practices. This complex modality of subjectless consent is the very opposite, the very destruction, of inclusion and of whatever entity or polity or community that would have the vile, brutal, murderous, expansionist, colonial intention to include or be included, where community attenuates rather than attends. Fuck the entire range of that portfolio when there's a mutual gravitational field, a regular influence, an ordinary nonlocality that keeps on gracefully falling, admitting of no prior separation but insisting, as Denise Ferreira da Silva says, on differing all the time. Meanwhile, the sovereign body is the incarceration of difference. It plays and replays itself as individuated mourning for lost community like a hambone made of plastic. There's a deep commitment to the settler's vicious longing for welcome and poets can make it sound as good as artists can make it look. To move out, then, in the flesh, towards the way of all things. In terrific pain, in terrific empathy, Spillers says, which Amiri Baraka will have come to feel in town, something in the way of things on their way away, destination out. His largesse is depressive because it moves at and then over the subject's, which is to say the poet's limits. He wonders if he's done anything at all in and through the Imam's prophetic commitment to naming, which emerges from the separation that seeing bears. Something in the *weidh* of things, where this mutuality in seeing (I see it; you see it, too) bears, somehow, the source of a division between the one who sees and names and the one who, in merely seeing, is relegated in the end to the merely seen, as if the violence of black looking within the frame—as it were—of the interior intersubjective, "the natal community," as Spillers calls it, will have been resolved, finally, in brutal recoil. Aimé Césaire speaks of a right to personality right as he's about to rock the party. If sometimes we can't help but say "what about me?" then Spillers says let us selflessly help us with that.

7.

Can difference without separation survive realness? Only, perhaps, if realness is productively misunderstood as passing through, rather than passing as, the real, which is to say as its im/possibility. What if, on the one hand, there really is nothing like the real thing and, on the other hand, there really is nothing like the real thing? No desert, just bottom, where real thing is as practically redundant as sweet thing: the real *res*, the *res res*, it's a *res* thing, this real thingliness, which is suitable, in its repetition, for persuasion. The question of what it is to got to be real is bound up with the question of what it is to be a thing among things. But this problematic of passing through the real, or all around it, which is movement through the general problematic of the law of genre in order to think its recomposition, its improvisation, but in a richly redoubled and real-ass way such that every invocation of the real is, as in Aretha's cover, which gives premature birth, as it were, to Marvin and Tammi's original, a *surreal*, unreal, covering and uncovering and recovering and discovering of it. Therein would lie a declaration that there's no such thing (as that static/statist conception), that there ain't nothing like that, that in passing through the real thing, which is nothing like the real thing, we become no-things, or what Silva calls "no bodies against the state," in their exhaustion of im/possibility.

8.

What if entanglement is a consequence of the idea of photoelectric wave-particle duality and quantum mechanics that actually troubles that duality and, then, those mechanics? If space-time and its laws go off a little bit at the subatomic level, such paralegality here indicating a dance whose black queerness turns out to refuse any sense of separation between the very small and very large, then how do we judge their realness? Maybe we just pass through the slits in it, the propulsive and repulsive contact between the classical and the quantum having required us to suspend judgement in a general sense or, at least, fastidiously to qualify every judgment with J. S. Bell's acronym *fapp*, which is, *for all practical purposes*, just a Scottish version of the Ohio Players' *Fopp*. And even then, what if there's a more general and practical social and aesthetic purpose to which this ritual caveat is inadequate? What if entanglement not only problematizes the idea of (wave-particle) duality (understood as a system, as a composite mental apparatus) but of prior separation and discretion, as well? (Here, I know that I am either radically misunderstanding or radically disturbing or simply obsessively applying even Bell's deconstruction of the opposition of system and apparatus, his dissatisfaction, ultimately, with the constitutive/decisive power that is given to measurement and the concomitant reduction of thinking to measurement if one desires to consider that nonlocality tends to revive Parmenides's dictum that it is the same thing to think and to be.) What if, then, we are allowed and required to think the concepts of wave, or particle, of wave-particle duality, as apparatuses rather than as systems in/of physical reality; so that the *very conceptualization* of that which is to be measured is itself an apparatus (that is constitutive of the very activity) of measurement? What if the richness and complexity that the appeal to duality is meant to preserve can only be preserved in movement through that duality so thoroughgoing that it destabilizes the very idea of measurement through which (that) duality is instantiated? What if there's an anomic animus that throws off iambic stride—the disruption of a normative dispensation or allotment or apportionment or measure? Immeasurable, uncountable number. A wronging or wringing of the word. An essential and constitutive criminality in the word, the immeasurable from which measure flows, verse fugitive both from itself and freedom, thereby disregarding every prosaic and presidential precedent. The (meta) physics of fascism is this: absence of choice given in the proliferation and imposition of irrelevant choices. Let's take a time out from all that. Recess: to escape discretion either as the determination of the observer or as the self-determination of the observed (structured in whatever opposition/ relation of wave and particle). The break, the hollow, the holler, the ditch, the dungle, the good foot, the mutron.

9.

Poetics is the difference between whatever it is that you think you have to say and whatever it is that language does; or, poetics is the relation, and the difference, between content and form; or, poetics thinks and enacts the differences that constitute the relation between content and form; or, poetics thinks the content and form of differentially inseparable nonrelation. Can you say all that with an accent gravity? For example, Claudia Rankine has an auditory signature, a sound (the microtonal oscillation between defeat and its deferral), but does she have a poetics? *Citizen* is an exhausting, exhaustive proof that the citizen is exhausted; it follows from *Don't Let Me Be Lonely*, which proves the impossibility, radical undesirability, and irreducible loneliness of sovereignty and the underprivilege of self-possession. But is it a proof or a restatement of a proof? An iteration of the already proven that doesn't so much make it more stylish or succinct but, rather, signs it, or, in another sense, takes up the assignment of signing for it, or co-signing for it, sharing a kind of investment in the subject/citizen's melancholic attachment to itself as loss (of power). Rankine has something (else) to say about a seemingly general and unavoidable cathexis to the impossible and the undesirable. Perhaps what's at stake is that evidentiary, postconceptual, forensic thing: let me write you a song about all that fucked-up shit you did. I'll put it in blue notes and vengeance-broken, aNourbeSean anguish and cross you. But can I cross you without crossing over? We both at the airport—why wouldn't you like that shit as much as me? I don't mean to be mean; I know you mean well. But what if eating the *Wall Street Journal* commits to a kind of initiatory ingestion in order to prove a point that ain't worth proving, another evidentiary gesture towards what we already know? When will knowing what *they've* done as how *we* feel reach the point where it no longer needs to be proved, insofar as it's never been (anything even close to that simple)? Why do we continually submit ourselves to this trial, an endlessness for which we volunteer, as an application for admission? When will we break free of the annular advancement and critique of this restrictive notion of the evidentiary? Sometimes it feel like we tired of feeling like that. But can we imagine imagining what exists? Can we get to the imaginary evidence of our shared practice? Why can't we see or hear that we'll never see or hear our inanimate and objectified bodies within the aesthetico-juridical frame? Rankine's generosity comes in taking these questions on as if they were hers alone, as if they were inscribed upon her person or essential to her own unique description. To address these questions, by way of a rendering of them that would be precise enough to unask them, requires escape from the critique of judgment. There's still something left to give up—the desire to be seen in order to see; the desire to ingest in order to expel; the desire to indict and pass sentence. Hand in and out of hand on the other hand, the jurisgenerative mobilizes imaginative evidence outside the aesthetico-juridical frame. And so, we have to sing this song that Rankine has all but surreptitiously written called "On nothing in *Citizen*," which is the dispossessive nonlocality of a dispossession, the poet's and the poem's disappearance into an essay on poetics.

10.

See, there's a recess in *Citizen*, an invitation Rankine extends. Recess is where the music, the music-poetry, the *mousiké*, comes from. Poetry finds; poetry founds; out of (airy) nothing, poetry finds and founds nothing at all. Is there a logic of poetic discovery, an analyric of entanglement, that is not in memoriam of identity? A poetics of the unparticular? It's not that there's nothing more or nothing new to be said about antisociality (i.e., the crowded but solitary anti- and ante-vestibular stall wherein [white] selves brown-move-in-brown-study themselves between mutually assured destruction and mutually destructive realization). It's that nothing, more and new, need be said. Poetry is not for something else to be said about things. Poetics is not the bridge between whatever someone has to say and the fact that something else is said. Nothing more and new need be said. Poetry is recess. It says nothing, in praise of nothing, constantly, serially, fugally. If you think this is all nonsense, you flatter me to the point of my disappearance.

11.

Nonsense is erratic trajectory, erotic in its refusal of narrow representations of representation, and with the complex play of nothingness through thingliness (the paraontological/anexistential field wherein the distinction between nothing and everything is constantly improvised). Blackness is situated in the sensuality of the nonsensical rather than in the already given supersensuality of the epidermal. Insofar as the critique of authenticity (paradoxically) asserts a right of (proprerty-in/as-)individuation in the (real) world, it is often nothing more than a disavowal of exsensual, consensual, nonsense, which is not just one difference among others but is, more precisely, the folded/fruited plain of a general difference both theorized and enacted as world's earthly and annihilative surrealization. Consider that the supposed relation between color and sense is often treated as a sociological matter. That's how we study, for instance, the ways that epidermal differences (which are manifest not only in the color but in the volume of one's skin) have been so often aligned with having or not having sense, betraying pigment's conceptual detachment from what it is supposed to mark, which allows it to be deployed as uniform, livery, garment, and name. Under this constraint, the analytic—as well as the counter-analytic—of the epidermal elides what it also illuminates. Sharing the social costs that attend epidermalization and distributing the benefits that accrue to sense's irreducibly material and differential supplementarity are entangled. They can be spoken of in terms of privilege and precarity despite the fact that the (color) line between them must be drawn with imprecision. When privilege is understood simply to accrue to a supposedly unmarked, paradoxically bare, whiteness, it is not only privilege but also whiteness—which is situated at the intersection of good sense and murderous brutality—that is misunderstood. The operation within which I am held, to and by which I am given, into and out of which I am (un)folded; and the particular impersonation from which the sounds you hear right now derive, which I would associate with illicit seeing, with multiple sensing, with black theory, which is to say theory, with black history, which is to say history; are (in the) nonsensical. Nonsense is sometimes manifest as a kind of happiness; and this capacity to be happy, to celebrate, is the condition of possibility of criticism's necessary unhappiness. What we have, insofar as we give it away, lets us know what, and under what conditions, we should have. What we have, and what we should have, is nothing other than the consensually nonsensical generality of a recessive trait, by way of which the poet retreats into (giving way in having given away) the hesitant sociality and sociology of blackness and poetry.

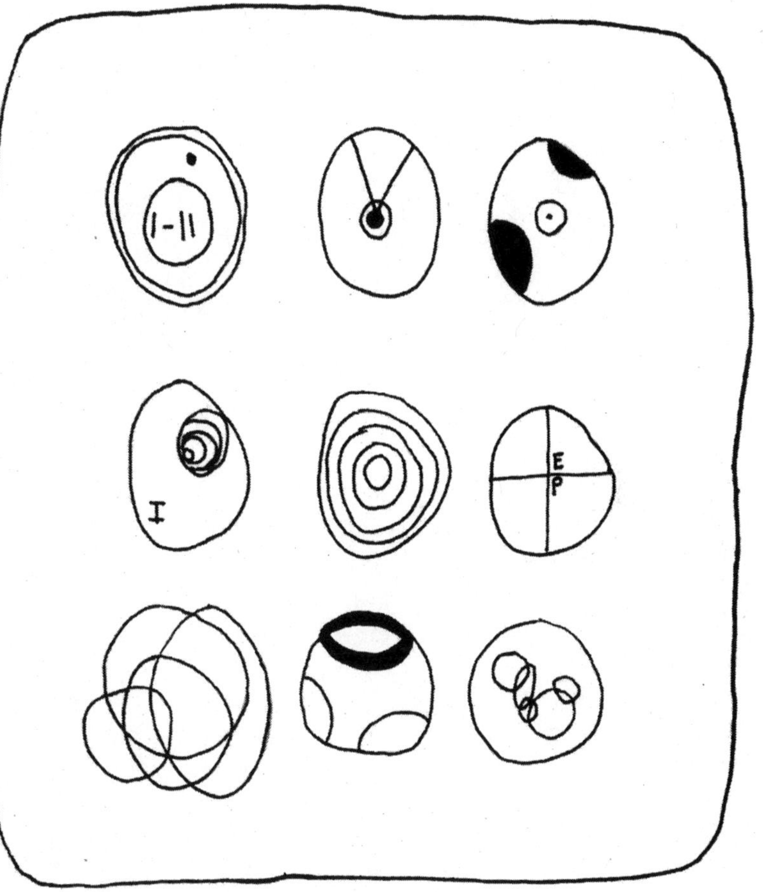
I-II
I
E
P

WHAT IS AN AFTERWORD?   *Mónica de la Torre*

The dictionary, from now on here referred to as the word book, doesn't have a fleshed-out entry for the word that refers to the words that come after the words of others, in the context of a publication, commonly in the form of prose commentary. Instead of a definition, the word book provides us with a synonym, the word *epilogue*, as well as a list of other synonyms at the bottom of the entry that includes the words *addendum, appendix, codicil, excursus,* and *supplement*. If it is almost comedic that these other words are themselves provided as addenda to the word *epilogue*—proving that when it comes to words, definitiveness is an illusion—, it is not coincidental that some of them, having medical and legal usage (and sounding like over-the-counter drugs), put us in mind of forensics.

Now, as obvious as it may seem, it bears mentioning that by *we* I mean *you* who are reading these words and *I* who has written them for you to read, joined temporarily on the page almost supernaturally, yet disjointedly, since contrary to appearance, we cannot be here at the same time. *Flesh is the threshold that speaks and that is called upon whenever you refer yourself to me, or I to you* (Anaïs Duplan). It also bears mentioning that this was not the case for the words you have read in this book up until this point, which were first delivered by poets, in the flesh, to an audience listening to them while they were being spoken. Everybody was in the same room, in a sort of unscripted choreographic arrangement. *"This dance is where we must now live,"* she continued, *in her bright confident tone* (Wayne Koestenbaum).

My words, intended for you to take in through your eyes instead of your ears, come much after the occasion in which the words of others were spoken. In that sense alone, they do constitute an afterword. The distance between that pre-pandemic moment and this one feels so vast at this time, that it is almost as if we needed a word even more bottomless than *after*, a small word designating seconds, months, decades, and geological eras alike. Yet what makes an afterword an afterword is not merely a temporal matter. The words in the next paragraph, and the ones following it, do not serve as the afterwords of the words here, not only because most of them have been written by the same author, me, intermittently signaled by the appearance of the first person singular, but also because they will not summarize what I have said before them. Rather, they will continue on the path that what I am saying now leads me to, which at this point is in the process of being discovered. *Poetry finds; poetry founds; out of (airy) nothing, poetry finds and founds nothing at all* (Fred Moten).

Neither, most importantly, will my afterwords summarize what anybody else has said. Despite what the word *summary* might suggest, with the word *sum* embedded in it as a reminder of the noun's proximity to matters of arithmetic, it entails *reducing* complex ideas and arguments presented in writing or speech to a set of so-called talking points that are subject to being easily paraphrased or repeated. *If mathematics like money and markets summon zero morality* (Ken Chen). Summing up is the opposite of adding to what oneself or others have said by responding and elaborating further, or better yet, by exploring the thoughts their words contain, in the company of those who've spoken them or someone else, in the act of being engaged in a conversation which requires at least two parties taking turns to speak, regardless of the lapse or delay between each party's speech or the forms it might take.

Let us return to the word book for a moment. Besides providing alternatives, it tells us what we already know: that the word referring to the words that come after a particular group of words considered the main body of a publication is simply a compound of the words *after* and *word*. If we dwell on these words briefly, we can go beyond what we already know we know about them and consider a few other things that the words taken separately evoke when put together. As we've seen, when the word *after* appears as prefix, the implication is one of mere temporal succession (suggesting the possibility that, by same logic, there could be beforewords and synchronouswords). *After* can also play the role of a preposition, as in the phrasal verb "to go after." What might it mean to go after words?

We might go after words when we think someone has mobilized words against us, when they have ugly histories, when we think they're misleading us or leaving something out, when they tell half-truths or box us in. We might go after them in order to seek reparation or redress. *We need caption-like material so history doesn't get lost* (Ariel Goldberg). In these cases, however, we're actually going after those who have used or are using the words, not after the words themselves, for words themselves cannot be at fault even though no word is innocent.

If we consider the traits of words themselves and not of those who use them, other possibilities open up. We might go after words simply because there's something we'd like to put into words and the words aren't coming to us. And/or, we could go after words because, as all of us who use words know, words have a very particular ability to elude us. Much effort goes into their capture, and even when captured, their fleetingness and endless circulation does not end. Words are everywhere and nowhere at once. Unrecorded, they scatter and morph, before fading into silence and memory and occasionally popping up in our dreams. *I tried, every night, to write down what they were saying, but their voices became softer, blurred together, and I realized I never got further than cleaning* (Brandon Shimoda).

We put words on paper and/or screens to give them provisional arrangements that emulate our mind's pathways in the process of arriving at them in the form of crystallized thought. We work on words we call ours so they behave the way we want them to, and although we may own up to our words, we never own them or have much control over them.

Compulsory legibility. Coercive intelligibility. Coercive legibility. Compulsory intelligibility (Myung Mi Kim's words fled this volume, for her words, perhaps, would have been coerced into an unwanted legibility). Words resonate. They belong to everyone and no one at the same time, and their centrifugal energy is reactivated again and again as soon as anyone comes into contact with them, whether they've been recorded or are being uttered on the spot. *The omnitexts that vibrate everything* (Tracie Morris).

Poets are especially aware of this, as evinced in the words before my words, making it pointless to try to offer an afterword attempting to arrive at some sort of conclusion on poets' thoughts on the words of poets that appear in the form of prose. And I am one of them too. Plurally and musically and lovingly and lucidly the reverberating words you have encountered before my afterwords circle around the notion that there is no such thing as the last word, but rather, a delirious and marvelous excess. *Let's hold on tightly to the belief that we have a right, not just to survive, but to live excessively, to reclaim that excess that has been stolen* (Raquel Salas Rivera). Instead, I offer these afterwords as an *ensayo*, a word that in Spanish refers both to the essay form and to the rehearsal of a performance. Why not call this performance an ongoing play, one that by the time my words reach you, began long before. In this play, *better than the projected or planned one* (Dorothea Lasky), your thoughts and their thoughts and my thoughts entangle and tango together in the space of this book on poets' words moving across the page that is a… *a field, a playground to observe the limits and boundaries, the shapes of our thoughts* (Cecilia Vicuña). With this I wrap up, since this book is a magical artifact with the peculiarity of being both bound and open even when it is closed.

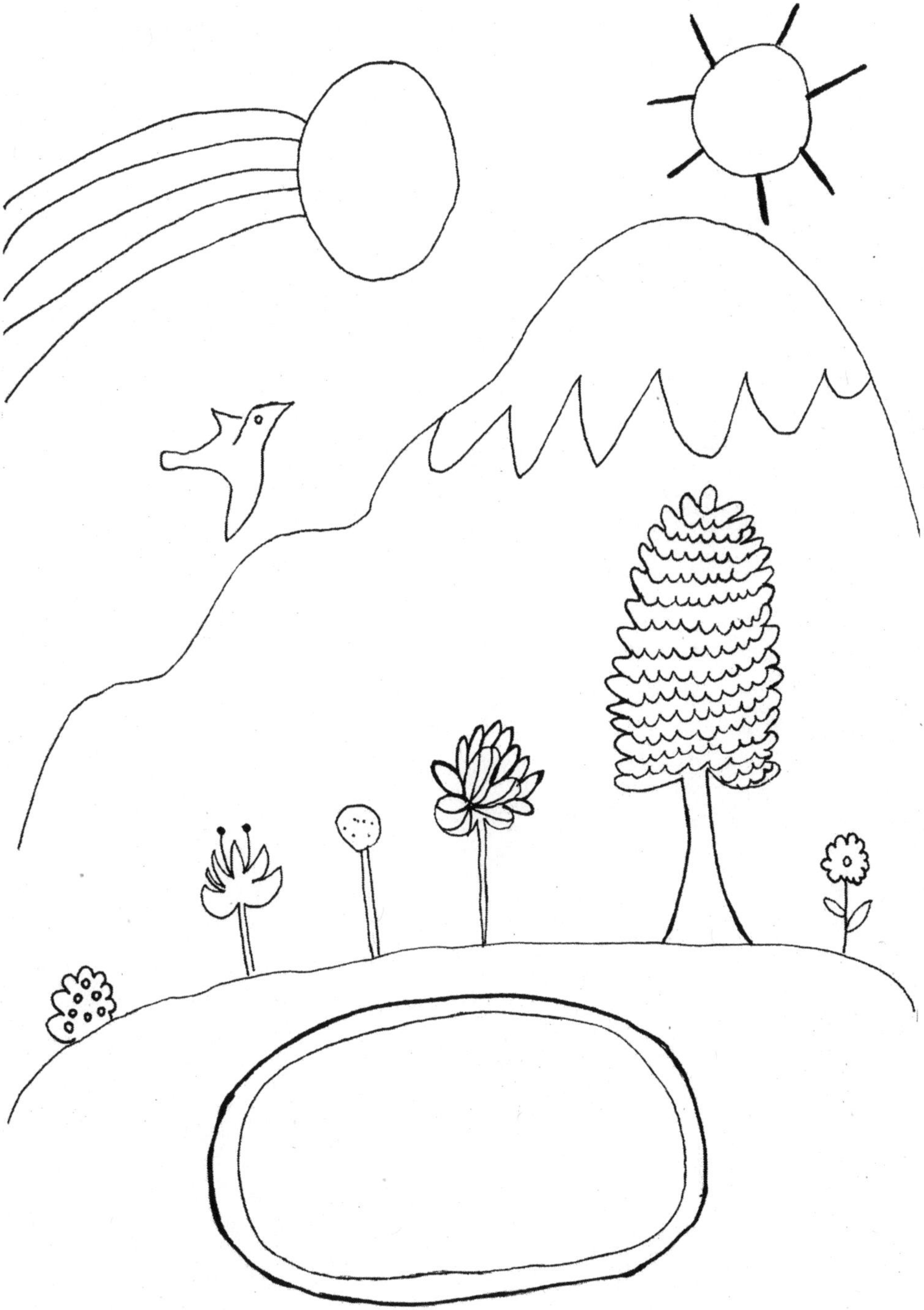

THE POET'S ESSAY Q&A – TRANSCRIPTION

Fred Moten

Q: Maybe just a general view, everyone here seems to be used to this mix of poetry and theory, but maybe just your take on it? And one thing that I thought is unusual in your writing, or also from other people who use the same method, is that you're also addressing the readers, or the listeners. You're saying "I" and "if you understand" and "if you listen", so maybe just if you can say something about that method, and the unusualness of combining the highly philosophical ideas with personal address?

FM: Well, I don't know, I just grew up in a neighborhood where that's how people talked…(laughs)…No, it's just…and I also, you know…I mean I would say that what I just read, you know, is an academic essay. Which is to say, you know, I have a job, and I work in the University, and they call me a teacher. And I've been trying really hard to figure out how to do that, and over the last two or three years I realized that the best way to do that is to not do that. But nevertheless, you know I be trying to talk with my students, and we try and talk about things. And I usually talk too much, and I'm trying to figure out how to not do that. But everything I've ever written pretty much for the last twenty five years has been in preparation for teaching, which has been, therefore, preparation to try to talk with people, which too often turns into talking to people. But I'm working on that, you know. And when I say it's academic, I really mean it in this very specific sense, which is that the academy is kind of a...it's a project for people who can't afford to live where they live. (Laughs.) You know, I don't know. Will I still be academic when I go home tonight? I don't know. I live at NYU. It's like, I don't know if Imma' ride a cab or if Imma' take the subway, but how far away do I have to get from Columbia to not be in the Academy? Are all the people who got displaced from Harlem no longer in the Academy, or are they, in fact, utterly held within the Academy? You know, I don't know. I mean, that inside-outside thing is, it's problematic. And to recognize it as problematic is not, I think, to indulge in despair, it's just to...sometimes I feel like these analytics that we have about the academic versus the non-academic, they have the same level of kinda...precision as chemotherapy, you know? They burn up what they supposed to heal. You know? And somehow that inside-outside thing ends up working as a kind of combination of cancer and chemotherapy, you know? And so, I just feel like...everything is much more complicated, and requires a much higher level of precision. Whereas, wherein, and by precision, I mean, you know, lyricism. So, I'm just blathering, I mean I don't know. I'm trying to answer your question. I don't know, I mean it's like...We all just...I just don't see anything that we don't need, you know? So, we need a lot of different ways to talk. And we really need to be able to, to hang out with one another, and hear all those different ways that people have to talk. So it's just another way to talk, you know? And, maybe it'll be helpful to somebody. So, just doing the best I can. (Laughs.) You know?

(Audience applauds.)

Q: I hate asking questions, so this is so ironic. Well, first of all, an observation that I already shared with Ken, which is that this building is so crazy because when you look out the window, it's like Columbia created a constellation from the lights, so it's like they made the sky as well as the land, but anyway. Sorry, I got really nervous all of a sudden. So, I just have a question, sort of building on your question, which is how do you listen? Because I love listening to you, but how do you listen? Because you have to listen to write, right?

FM: It depends on who you ask because, if you go to my house and ask them, they probably say not very well. (Laughs.)

Q: Yeah, but that's what I mean, it's situational. Listening is situational, right?

FM: I mean…See, the trouble is…the trouble is, there's like a thing that happens you know, where you feel almost like a kind of…a sense of accomplishment that borders on hubris, and it kinda comes with this feeling that you have of being able to answer any possible question… (laughs.) It's terrible, it's like a horrible thing. So, I feel like I can answer your question, you know? I mean, and make it seem good, you know? But I don't know. I'm trying to learn. I know that there have been, you know, I just, I grew up in a house that was filled with music and my mom was really into Jazz, and I've read a lot of things that Jazz musicians say about the necessity of listening and the inseparability of listening and playing, that these are kind of a steady state system, in a way. That to play, is to listen. Or to play well, is to listen well. And it's a kind of… an almost…it's like a fundamental kind of responsiveness, you know? An openness and vulnerability. Again, you know Karen Barad will call it response-ability. This absolute, so to speak, ability to respond. And so, I could say…all I can really say is that that's maybe…that's what I aspire to, but I know I'm not even close, you know. So, really actually, in my house, they would tell you [that I listen] badly and I pretty much have to say the same thing, but I'm trying to learn how to listen better, and I hope I do. (Laughs.) I hope I do. I'm trying. I'm essaying, you know. Which is now officially a verb in the English tongue.

Q: Thank you so much, it was so beautiful. I'm wondering, you spoke about dispossession, and this dissatisfaction, and I'm wondering how they both, in your mind, played out in poetic language, in poetic form, and how you express or celebrate dispossession, or even radical loss, as it comes to identification and all the subject deterioration.

FM: Well, I think maybe when I use the word dispossession, I'm kind of always in my mind seeing it in my mind with a little line or a slash or something between the prefix, you know, and the root, in the sense that…I mean…Look, I mean, there's a very specific way in which I could sit up here and say, "Well, being Black in America, I have this experience, or I have this trace, this mark…on my body, or in my person" and it's a mark which ultimately undermines any kind of claim I would actually have to having a body or having a person, being a person, and at that mark comes from what it means literally, to have been property, you know? And I could make this claim as if it were a special claim, but it's only difference I suppose would be maybe I have much smaller access to anything that will allow me to think that I can't make that claim. And there's a lot of people running around thinking that they don't have the ability to make that claim, but they just haven't thought about it hard enough yet, ok? You know, it's like a Macbeth formulation…man that is born of a woman, or something like that. But given that I can't disavow that claim, which is a claim on nothing, which is a claim on being unable to claim, a claim on being unable to have, a claim on being radically dispossessed of the very capacity to possess, you know? Insofar as I can't *not* make that claim, I bear it, with the intention of sharing it, ok? Because, for me, that claim is to condition a possibility of another way of living on the earth. That's not owning it, but just trying to walk around gently on it, *as* it. So, in this respect, you know…it is also about the terror and the horror of having to claim being possessed. Right? Which I don't take lightly, or want to talk about it as if it were some easy thing. It's a terrible thing. You know what I mean? It's a terrible thing to be the descendants of those who are possessed, and to have to claim being possessed. Okay? I can't think of anything more horrific. But I can't think of anything more likely to continually produce the chance of, you know, what Cecilia was calling emergence. So, you know. That's what we got. That's what I have to give, is not having. (Laughs.) You know? That's all I got, that's all I can share.

Q: It makes me feel like crying to hear you, but your laugh wakes me up. You laugh so beautifully. It's just heartbreaking. But hearing you, I didn't want to be one asking a question, but I couldn't stop myself. It's your use of the word "recess"...Hm? Just speak some more of that choice, "recess."

FM: Well, it's got a double edge to it, in the sense that it can mean a break, a stop, a...what's the word? A ceasing. A time for play. Like recess in school. But it is also, I think...I mean I think about it topologically...a low place, a hollow, or as they might say in Appalachia, a holler, you know? Which therefore, implies, also a sound. A topographical sounding. Which is also a descent, a deepening. All those things for me are there. And you can hear it in the music all the time. It's like...well, you know, James Brown is the great musician of the one, that downbeat. But I always thought that it would be more accurate that every time he talks about the one or being on the one, he's really talking about being on the zero. (Laughs.) The one is just this sort of utterly temporary, conceptual scheme, from which one looks back on that which can't be named. Which is that, that recess, that nothingness. It's just a thing where you listen to it, you listen for it, and you know for me, that's where we...I was gonna say that's where we are, and then I was gonna say that's where we come from, but maybe the best way to put it is that's where the difference between where we are and where we come from doesn't signify. But, I mean, you know about it. (Laughs.) You've been doing it forever right, and I mean that, you know, I mean forever. You've been doing it before you got here. So that's what we do, that's how we do, you know? So. Alright.

Ken Chen, Ariel Goldberg, Wayne Koestenbaum

DL: Let's welcome the three of you up here to this very handy table. We have a little bit of a question-and-answer phase of our conversation. And I thought I'd start it up with just a question, but this is really open for the audience to ask questions. So just, keeping with the theme, I thought that each of you could maybe talk about what logic, meaning, and memory mean to you, especially in the creation of your piece for today? And or anything else you want to incorporate into that. Ariel? You want to go first? You don't have to, but.

AG: Sure, why not…Logic?

DL: Meaning, memory, some kind of combination? Aesthetics could be incorporated.

AG: Yeah, so, I'm excited about all the resonances, too, between all of our presentations, so I'm sort of catching all of those in my memory of what just happened. But I moved kind of quickly and impressionistically through some materials, that maybe if I just say I'm really interested in writing about a place and a time in relationships that I wasn't personally, you know, in real life, there. Like, I wasn't born in the 70s, so I think I'm dealing with both the sort of lassitude and the fluidity of how one must rely on imagination and fantasy to access those places, and also the sort of desire I have for accuracy and for representation through whatever writing I do that honors the people who were there. And I think one of the roadblocks is, you know, like Betty Lane who is one of the photographers whose work I showed, she passed in 2012. And then the other photographer whose work I was talking about, Joan Biren, she's still living, so there's challenges for each of them in terms of how one co-authors memories, and memories become hybridized based off of the dissonant voices that are constructing them, and the meaning is, I think, I hope that it's flexible and varies based off of interpretation. So, that's sort of, you know, it's like the movement class for crocus, sort of like (laughs) awkwardly, fantastically, but also seems to be a means of survival.

KC: When I started writing poetry, I tried to write some poems that were using operations of reason, and I think it might have been inspired by the LSAT (laughs). But also, there's classical Chinese poetry where if you just look at the characters it reads like logic problems, like *if the moon did not know longing, it would always stay round.* Or, *if the gods had desires, they too would age.* So, I thought that was cool. But then, in retrospect, having written a lot of that stuff a long time ago, it occurred to me that maybe I wrote through reason because I didn't feel, maybe it came out of insufficiency? Or, feeling like I couldn't write like the more normal lyric poem that was all about myself, so I could go to reason. In my previous poems, there are these points where the logic keeps breaking down, and it's like a critique of logic. But then, in reading about the history of colonialism, of course you learn about the role of reason…you know, knowledge is power, etc, etc. So I was thinking about how I could reuse those same structures, but in ways that maybe were saying something that was both more political, but also more metaphysical. And maybe two more specific things that inspired me: there's a great poem by NourbeSe Philip that's on YouTube. I don't actually remember the name of it right now, but she keeps doing this thing where she keeps changing the words, and it's almost like a computer program and it's one of the best things I've ever read on language and power. And, what was the second thing I was going to say?…Yeah, so I guess that's sort of where I came into this.

WK: As I listen to these, my response will be kind of comparative. So, I was interested in three prosodies, just to generalize a little bit. I mean I'm struck very much in yours, Ken (turns to KC) about like, so-called "anaphora"; but "if." Particularly the passage with "if this, if that," "if this and so this," so I think stacking is what I might have said when I began. As I heard that, you were using a prosody of stacking to get at something that part of an essay, the essay part of that, there actually was material that could be unearthed and it would be unearthed through the investigation of the stacking. And I think Ariel, (turns to AG) in yours there was something about like assembling, as I heard it, in a way the material that got lost through the glossy magazines, contracts, or through the air-conditioned archivist room. That moving through the slivers of material was a way to find things that you wouldn't know. And I think in my procedure in that way, to get at the logic meaning, I think was using the structure of plausibility, or implausibility, as a kind of plastic material, and to move forward in an investigation superficially fictional, through testing out, using syntax to test out, in each sentence, the edges of plausibility and implausibility. And to use the inner drama and vertigo of that negotiation of like, is this sentence going to…you know, which side do I even want to be on? Plausible or implausible. To move to material that I wouldn't find my way to otherwise, or consider mine to find. Not claiming any kind of alchemic or divinatory powers, but that using structures that aren't maybe, you know, whether from anaphora to syntax's ability to float plausible and implausible things by just suspending the sentence, as a way to enlarge one's powers of finding.

DL: And I was just thinking a little bit more about memory and thought we could talk about it, which related to what everyone's saying and thinking about, obviously the image of the father or, you know, the figure that is maybe coming undone and going to look for that person in the underworld, and this idea of the caption, or the ephemera, the letter to the editor: all the things that kind of get thrown away or taken away, or not kept, not preserved, not archived. And then, thinking of crocus potentially as a symbol for memory? I'm not sure what we would say (laughs) but just that idea of memory as this thing that we long for, we long to keep, we long to preserve, you know, there's a source of anxiety if we were to lose it. You know, that memories would just kind of fade away. And so maybe that's the idea behind history, in some way. And so, I guess the question for you all is, just thinking about writing your piece, do you feel that we always lose memory, or do you think memory is something that is preserved...(laughs) this is a very serious table... or answer whatever you want, but (laughs) I feel like we're maybe at the UN or something, it's this table...But, anyway, maybe start with (turns to AG)...you want to start again? You're right here. But whoever wants to can start!

AG: (Laughs) I'm gonna pass to you...(turns to KC).

KC: Sure...Yeah, memory. I feel like talking about this is making me realize how my process is so dialectical and how a lot of what I'm doing is kind of refuting how I used to write. And I used to think that poetry was about "What is your self?" and "What is the most meaningful thing you have to say?" and how can you write something that was very pure about what is your self, what do you remember. But then once I did that, I felt that there was something kind of selfish (laughs)...No pun intended. And I thought, well, how can I write about stuff that is external? Or political or historical or impersonal or meaningless, if the thing that seems meaningful is subjective. And so I tried to read about everything (laughs) that happened in the last five hundred years, which hasn't worked out very well.

But it's also very difficult for me to write because, at the end of the day I still write in a way that's very subjective, and so part of it is how can I write about an impersonal or historical memory if my mode is still about personalization, or subjectivity of writing? And so, part of it is about memory in that it is setting down what actually did happen in the past. But there's another part, if we're thinking about what you're saying (turns to WK) and about...the harpsichord actually! When I wrote this piece, there was another twenty pages and at some point I just had to stop, and it reminded me of Baroque harpsichord, where it could just go on forever, you know? Like you just start the song and it keeps playing. There is this "if/then" domino effect falling. And for me I was thinking about "if/then" as both this logical condition, and when you read all the political history, it is all sort of like—because of the access to coal in England, England could start the Industrial Revolution. Because of the Haitian Revolution, Napoleon sold the Louisiana Purchase to America. It's all a series of "if/then" statements, and so at one point I was like if I could write "if/then statements," I could summarize the entire history of the world, that would be pretty cool. But then it was like a little bit too haunting. (Laughs) But I also thought about "if" as speculation, history as this never-ending series of alternate fantasy-histories. Like the Crusaders thinking if only we could convert China to Christianity, then China would declare war on the Turks and the Persians and then we could have a unified Christendom. "If" as a memory that never happened, where something is constantly being displaced…you lose labor somewhere so that you get it somewhere else, you lose this source of resources, you get it somewhere else. The more I read about history, the more I see alternate histories and this constant "if." Like you probably all know about Japanese American concentration camps here, but it came very close to interning Korean Americans during the Korean war, like I think there was even a law that was passed, but then it was just never executed. Or before 9/11 we were on the verge of passing this huge law against hate crimes, and then a few days later 9/11 happened and that was done. Or I have also read that when the Americans conquered Western Europe during World War II, Roosevelt was almost like, "You know, we should just stay here, that would be cool." (Laughs) I thought about how memory could have happened in a different universe, which generated a politics that seemed psychedelic and weird.

WK: The sense in which I would want to invoke memory in terms of this fables project is that the memory is the structures of tale telling and of linguistic structures from my earlier, earliest, encounters with language. You know, from birth onward. And that since as a kid I read fairy tales and as a younger person I wrote fiction and then became a poet and essayist, to return to a mode that is a way of moving through language that is my child self's way, but literally, it's as if the neurological structure of argumentation and fantasy that comes with this form of stretched tale telling, is a structure of linguistic making and of world making and perception that I don't remember, but I can step into as a navigational system again. So, it's a curious double-bodied sensation I have when I write these, that I'm not thinking about...I'm thinking just like I'm a grown up writing poems or essays, and I'm moving toward figuring out what it is that needs to be said today. But my process of navigation is this...just kind of...I don't know, there must be a structuralist and post-structuralist word for these...like the image repertoire of storytelling devices that are a kind of syntax that I can reinhabit, since it hasn't been aired in my life for so many decades. It has the rustiness and truth-telling capacity of things in archives that haven't been tampered with or corrected over the years. So, it's the memory of the device, it's the memory that the navigational device has, not the memories that I put into the box of the piece.

AG: Well, I don't know if this is going to be a swerve from crocus's land, and also the maps and thinking, trying to hold 500 years and more. But I think that my motivation, I've been told by readers, friends, of the messy drafts of whatever I presented today, that I need to explain to my readers or listeners why I care, or why I'm obsessing over these sorts of textural tendrils around photos, or why is accuracy so important, or what motivates the foraging that I'm doing and the fashion in which I'm presenting it. And, it's like I'm just so focused on "gather, now" because time is running out. Quite literally, like a lot of the photographers that...I'm writing a sort of photo history of lesbian and gay photographers from the last twenty-five years of the twentieth century. So, I would say, you know, more than a third of the photographers I'm interested in are no longer living, and the other ones are older. So there's that rush for memories, but then once you arrive...You know, I did an oral history with Jeb this summer, but the memories are not necessarily...factual...and that's really interesting. Or when I asked her about the nature of her lighting equipment in these photo shoots for her first book *Eye To Eye* she said, "I didn't bring lights," and I'm like, "Okay, well in the tape recording I hear all this lighting equipment going off, and there's a child talking about the lighting equipment." And then she's like, "Yeah, maybe I brought lights." So that was an interesting thing about the texture of memory. I think that I'm....you know, I just wrote this piece about the forms of contemporary photography, of which I had a screen grab from in my presentation, and I literally saw history being erased in some way. Where this curator was saying this photographer is unknown, and so I think there is this urgency around gathering information along the spectrum of truth/untruth accuracy/inaccuracy. And hopefully something comes out of it. Because, I think erasure of queer histories, Black feminist histories, is real, and I see it happening and it's sort of like, how to address it and also think about how archives are Western constructs. So, even dialoguing with *The New York Times,* where it's like, you didn't attend to the real issues of talking about trans people today, which is the epidemic of trans women of color being murdered, and they don't talk about that in their review of the exhibition that celebrates artists who are trans and genderqueer, etc. So there's a lot of that sort of tension and you know, what is the authority of the archive. I think on a personal level, in terms of family history, I don't have access to the vast majority of my family's history because of the Holocaust, because of trauma, because of literally records never being constructed. My mom doesn't have a birth certificate, for example, and she tried to find it. So, things like that are what motivates it on a personal level.

DL: I thought this could be a good time to open it up if people have questions. And we have this beautiful green taped microphone that I think, if you want to ask a question…I hope this doesn't make it scary…that you would go up there to…just so that, because we're being recorded…forever…The memory of this will never fade away. It could, but, at least not for the short present. Anyway, yes, would you like to ask a question?

Q: Yeah, there are two questions, two issues I'd like to raise. If I was going to offer an example of writing in this style that you described, I would suggest W.J. Cash's *The Mind of The South,* where he does what I think is a really great job of explaining the subtlety of social relations and the social psychology of the south and how slavery anchors itself in society. And I think he did it with his writing style, almost more than the logic of what he was doing…I spent most of my career writing research reports.

My stuff would never get through an editor if I wanted to do what you do. And so, I was wondering where that balance is? Between what I would describe as "verbal diarrhea" and…discursive analysis. The second question I want to ask is, you know, I've heard many many times that good writing is in the editing. How much editing do you do to produce pieces like you did? Does it just come out as a flow the way poetry sometimes emerges? I think poetry is edited as well…but how do you, what is the creative process in producing that kind of work?

KC: I love verbal diarrhea. (Laughs)

(Audience applauds, laughs.)

WK: I'll just say with editing…in terms of the spectrum of writing that one, that I've done, in my life, between writing that behaves more like what you're calling discursive analysis, and then the other stuff which I would certainly never call verbal diarrhea, but I would call…literature, or just a different kind of…(Audience laughs) No offense! But just it's not, that's not the way I would describe the vast realm of poetries and work that…that work, you know, editing per se the quality of, or the meaningfulness of an utterance doesn't…the amount of editing…there's constant editing of anything that gets produced. Including, I'm sure, factually everything that we've written is…but you know, again, it's not like you have to…I think it's…I remember the first time I was introduced to the notion of the "discipline" of creative writing, somebody wants that, the person who was in charge of inculcating freshman into this practice said something like, you know, about how important revision was. And of course, revision is important. It's important that like Tuesday happens after Monday and Wednesday after…The revision of moving forward in time has happened, but not as a sense of…the requirement for entrance into say ability or readability.

KC: I mean the irony is that a lot of the things I write are all about discursiveness actually, and there are also things I've written that aspire much more to be in the diarrhea track of the bipolar thing we described.

Actually, this thing took a lot of editing, it actually takes a lot more editing…There's certain things I write that use elements of discursive tropes. Like, you know, analytical reason. And it's actually much harder to write or edit, because it's like trapping yourself at each step because you have to use the contour of logical argument to keep going. So, those pieces are ones that actually end up being much more edited…You know, I have a lot of experience writing things that are very discursive, like grant applications, legal briefs and things like that. I'm not a lawyer right now, but the first time I starting writing as a lawyer, it was really mind-blowing to me. I think as a writer you aspire to find your voice and have some body language to your writing. And when you write things like a grant report or a lot of academic writing or legal writing, that all must be expunged. So, people used to say, "How did being a lawyer affect your writing?" and I used to say, "It really killed my soul but in like a really great way," because it almost became a kind of experimental writing? Because I was like, "Oh these lawyers just write like they're holding sledge hammers or something." It's just relentless argumentation, repetition and I was like, "Oh, maybe I can kind of treat that as an exotic literary style." And so I find that I've become more attracted to writing where there's clearly some kind of rigorous process going on, but it eludes my ability to paraphrase it, or summarize or translate it. So I feel like I'm increasingly attracted to things on the diarrhea side of the spectrum, because with a lot of poetry I can quickly assimilate it, and my ability to reason encompasses it too neatly. For me, the attraction is to try and understand something I don't understand.

AG: Well, I just wanted to say something briefly about process and editing and…I think that the editor can stand in as a metaphor for legibility, or this maybe false assumption that legibility is the goal. And that when writing in between genres, or playing with a prompt, like frolicking around in poetic lassitudes, you are committed to a certain degree of illegibility through cross-genre-ness. And that you can't please everyone, basically. And that editor is a subjective person, so it's this practice audience for who might read it or experience it, and a piece can change so much depending on who's editing it.

DL: Another question?

Q: This may be related to this conversation…It might be helpful if you could tell us what exactly you asked them to do?

DL: Well, I just asked all of the presenters to think about this prompt of the poem essay or the poet's essay. And just as I…I don't know if you were here in the beginning when I gave the introduction, but I talked about it as a class assignment, so it was kind of a similar thing, like a vague sort of term. But then obviously I organized them into what I thought would be good groups. They weren't necessarily thinking of their groups when they wrote their pieces. They didn't even know…it was all behind my, whatever, psyche. (Laughs.)

Q: Did you have access to the introduction that she gave us? Her thinking of it?

AG: Yes.

Q: For me, coming here I have been obsessed with the intersection between essay and poetry for quite a long time. Actually, more on the side of people who write "creative nonfiction." So, I think one of the things that came up just now, was the idea of…not so much logic, but maybe…I'm going to say the word coherence. I'm not saying that I didn't follow what you were saying. And also, having been in settings where people are talking about "fiction" and "structure" etc. etc., the idea of "narrative." So, this was great to begin this way. I'm just curious if there might be more of a discussion of…just, the use of these terms. And for me coming from the different environments where people think of them differently, and you all have different ways in which you write. Sorry for the long explanation, my name is Deborah Eater, I just want to mention that, but thank you all and could you maybe comment a little bit on what I said, if that makes sense?

DL: I think Tracie Morris, who is one of our presenters, wanted to say something.

TM: I'm not trying to get out of my lane or anything, but I just feel like, you know, maybe because I'm a teacher, but I'm being a little nurturing in defending my colleagues here. You know, coherence is a subjective thing, and I'm a little offended by the term verbal diarrhea because it implies scatological, and so, I think what we're talking about is convention. We're talking about convention, not coherence, convention. And I think for people who are used to conventional approaches to language, that this is a master class in thinking outside of your conventions to people who know what they're talking about. And know what they're doing, okay? And it's an opportunity to hear differently, I think all of us, all of this tells us what the world outside of our coffee klatsches and contexts understands what creative writing and innovation is. It's a very narrow bandwidth. But it's something to be embraced. It's not something that they need to feel defensive about, or justify because it's not what you're accustomed to, anybody's accustomed to, because of the narrow bandwidth of what people consider "professional creative writing." And I'm not saying you intended it that way, but that's what it gave off to me. And I'm not putting pressure on them to defend it, I'm just articulating how I felt and how I received some of those comments. So, it's like, how can we open it up so that people can receive different ways of approaching language differently? As opposed to…those are choices of word usages that you guys made when you say "coherence." I'm not saying that was your intention! Let me finish because I'm on the mic right now. I'm not saying that's not your intention, either of you, but I'm just, before we get into a lens of feeling like we have to justify innovative work, to just sort of hear it in an open kind of way. So, that's…does that make sense? I mean just, I don't want it to go on in that way because I'm not going to do anything, I don't think any of us are talking about conventionality in any way. So, I'm just putting that out there and if that's not your expectations, maybe this isn't the right context for you. But I suggest an openness of hearing as opposed to a presumption about whether or not the panelists know what they're doing, because they do.

DL: One thing is, Dean Carol Becker also wants to add to this conversation. (Laughs.)

CB: I take the power of the deanship to be here. (Laughs) No, no, I'm also a writer, so in this context I'd like to be the writer. I feel like, almost, and I'm going to build on what Tracie said a little, I think. It's almost as if Dottie, your concept doesn't…I think you have an even bigger ambition than changing our notion of what the essay could be, I feel like your ambition really is to change the notion of what reason can be, or how we understand reasonableness, or coherence, or integrity of thought. Because what you're all doing, what we heard just now, are people approaching the way in which the mind works, and the way in which the mind understands the world in unique ways, and that we live in a culture, a very utilitarian society, which has one way of understanding what is reason and reasonableness and coherence, to Tracie's point. So I feel like what we're really doing, when we talk about the poet's essay at some level, is you're saying, there are many ways to understand the world, and there are many forms of language that we don't attribute the ability to understand the world. We see them as something else, but in fact they're organizations of systems of thought as important to the way in which we are human, as what we think of as a conventional essay, or reasonable, so I'm just throwing that in there.

DL: Yeah, I love that. I agree with those points. Yeah, definitely hoping to challenge that and to challenge the scope. Because, I do think we take it for granted…I'm not supposed to be talking, but…We do take for granted this idea of the essay or the five paragraph essay, and that becomes a frame on our imagination. So hopefully this is getting you to think about that differently.

KC: Yeah, we can do kind of like a block of questions, so kind of make it less…adversarial.

DL: Yeah, sure! (Laughs.)

WK: People just say their thing.

DL: Yeah, maybe even two or three more people.

Q: I was struck by Professor Morris, what you were saying about this idea of convention, and thinking about convention as a mandate to cohere, or a kind of social imperative. And I was just wondering if maybe you could speak to the way that your work is envisioning a kind of social space, if it's relinquishing a relationship to convention, or a relationship to reason, sort of reimagining what a social space or anti-social space might look like?

Q: I just have some, kind of, thoughts I'll throw out, since it's like an open forum. One of the things I was thinking about with Ariel and Ken's reading was the idea of a fugue, I mean what you said, stacking is similar to the idea of just kind of returning and expanding, and also ties into what Professor Lasky was speaking about, with the idea of the essay is an opportunity to ask questions and to not know, as opposed to know. I mean, I think the more I interrogate myself the less I know, and the more I interrogate the world the less I know. So that's one of my thoughts for you to consider. And then the other one, is um, Michel Leiris, who I know you reference in your, um (points to WK) sorry to point…(Laughs).

WK: No, it's ok!

Q: …you reference in your writing, and Lydia Davis just did the new translation of *Scratches*, and I was just thinking about that, and we're talking about subjectivity. I think he's almost a master of the form, I suppose. So one thing I would ask is, just your ideas, to expand on your ideas of subjectivity and the world. And the last thing is, ideal forms. You know, I mention Leiris, but I am sure there are other people that you deeply admire and perhaps one of those things might be interesting to you to respond.

AG: What was that last bit?

141

Q: Oh, um, favorite versions of the form, I suppose would be a way to say it.

AG: I guess I can start off, this question over here was about social histories and landscapes if I'm remembering that correctly (turns to KC).

KC: (Turns to DL) Are we derailing your plan?

DL: Not at all! No, no, no! How about we respond to this, and then maybe we'll break.

AG: It's okay, and the idea of the fugue, which is really beautiful, and subjectivity. Ok, yeah, I think maybe I want to fold subjectivity into whatever essayistic writing that I'm doing about these photographic histories, and I think that I identify really strongly with Jeb, and I want to parse out that identification, even along its fissures. We're both, we come from, in terms of listing identities, very similar backgrounds as white middle-class Jewish lesbians and…(turns to DL) we're getting a time limit?

DL: Not at all!

AG: Okay.

(Audience laughs.)

DL: I was just talking to Ken, it was rude.

AG: Oh okay, it's fine, it's cool. And I think but also adding a trans perspective, and also trying to understand how, you know, certain versions of white lesbian feminist collectivities and political resistances failed, and how relationships and difference and not, you know, not having exact replicas of identities is a way to crack into thinking about coalition, and those are some of the things that are driving how I construct this piece and the quandaries that abound within it and speaking across history and thinking about how it relates to the present.

WK: Just it's striking me that an overall comment about everything, about this, is that language itself, and not to essentialize language across all the different languages that have been and will be and that are, but that the laws and behavioral gravities and tropisms of language, require a lifetime's listening and are very complicated and beautiful and are filtered through the histories of people who have used the language, the meanings, the formation of words, and that the larger responsibility I think that any writer or reader would feel, is not to any gatekeeper or any even notion of what a genre requires, but just to all the voices and prior auditions that are contained within language when allowed to do its thing, to some extent, and that I think that our role as linguistic, or as readers here, as linguistic investigators is to have a certain quietness and humility in the face of language's proverbial wiliness and to behave, not that it is, it doesn't know things, but it has temperatures and moods and prior knowledges and, I think that that is the editor to whom we owe fealty as well as the, in a way, the force of either correctness, or it's the ethical…I don't know what the word is…the judge to whom we who behave in language must listen to is the judge that adheres in language's wily procedures. I think.

KC: I wanted to add one more thing about (laughs) verbal diarrhea… I'm obviously a total fraud and dilettante, but I'd like to talk about a book I've only read part of, and how one origin of, you know, Western literature is in Rabelais. And the main character's born, I think, through his parent's anus and it's like a sea of shit, and I think how perfect is it that the origin of modern Western literature is scatological. And that's not a book that you see assigned that much, or read that much, but it is actually an exemplar of the essay form in that there's one part that's just a list of everything everyone's wearing, inventories. But it's all about shit. The problem with scatology is that it's excessive, and there's a surplus meaning that comes with shittiness. There might be some way to think about legibility or convention through Rabelais that might be really useful, and I wrote down "thank Tracie Morris" (laughs) with a heart around it. Um…

Q: What about balance? You're kind of overdoing it.

KC: Well, why not overdo it?

Q: What happens to that balance between editing, discursive analysis, and poetic subtlety?

WK: Balance isn't required of works of art. You don't say of Picasso that he should have had more Leonardo in him. You don't say of an outhouse that it should have more of a cathedral in it. (Audience laughs.) You don't say of a work by Wayne Koestenbaum that it should have more of… Dorothea Lasky in it. I pray that it could have some. (Audience laughs.) You don't make from outside the organism an integrity of a work of art or a person that created it, judgements about what it should hold or how it should be measured. That's an extremely closed and suspicious way of viewing the diversity of human articulation. That's the way I see it.

(Audience applauds.)

DL: That's a good place to end this portion. (Audience laughs.) But the good news is we have all day. I mean this is just the beginning. So I'm excited to see what happens next. If you come back in about fifteen minutes, it won't be perfectly fifteen minutes…but as close to fifteen as possible. We're going to hear about the essay, the manifesto, and the poetic imagination from Tracie Morris, Anaïs Duplan, and Raquel Salas Rivera, so we'll see you soon.

Tracie Morris, Anaïs Duplan, Raquel Salas Rivera

DL: Thank you so much, thank you to you three, and I thought like last time I could just ask a couple of questions and then we can open it up to the group. So, just for all of you, what I wanted to know how you felt the idea of a manifesto is both for, of, or against the imagination, and just that idea of why do we make manifestos? (Laughs.) Whoever wants to start.

AD: I think…I guess I think about manifestos as places where you can collect a body of ideas that then sort of leads to some further action for whatever reason. That those ideas are spurring action. And that can be, for whatever reason I'm thinking right now of "The Mundane Afrofuturist Manifesto," I think it's one of my faves. And it's sort of Martine Syms's undoing of all of the conventions that we know about Afrofuturisms. So, thinking about what is an Afrofuturism that's not in space, or that has nothing to do with galaxies or stars, or things, you know, if you pare it back, what remains. And then trying to sort of spur people to act out or maybe even to explore what those things are. Yeah, that's, I'll leave it at that.

RSR: I think sometimes we just have to say the thing. And, the affect of the energy of a manifesto is kind of that feeling of just having to say the thing. Except it's a little condensed. (Laughs.) But I also really believe that right within that framework, you can do a lot. Just as you can do a lot within any other genre, if you take genre to be a looser category, or genres to be looser categories, then you can take kind of like an affect and a feeling and you can run with it, and you can actually do a lot within it that makes it porous. So, I don't know if I'm good for defining it as much pushing against it.

TM: I agree with both of my colleagues here. I think, one of the speech acts, if you will, that we're talking back to is the banality of evil. You know? The sort of passive-aggressive bureaucratic horror of policy that destroys people. The manifesto is an assertive-passionate way of speaking against that, because it's a form of gaslighting, right? Ah, you didn't really see that, I didn't really say that, it's all, you know, shocking on, or whatever it is, it's all pithy, and it's said in this, you know, stentorian tone, and it's sort of "Oh." And then you go, "Wait, did I just, did they just throw a bomb, wait, what happened?" And so, the sort of normalization of harm that actually manifests in policy and law and also the things that are good about policy and law, lend themselves to, you know, "Did I just hear that?" Whereas the manifesto is unequivocal in the way that one hears. I think one of the things that's interesting, sorry to be Austin's stand-in here, but you know the way that he talks about law is important in the way that he frames law as a form of doing, not just describing. And Ken and I were having a great conversation about that. I was pre-law, he actually processed it and became a lawyer. But how in some way, through law and through poetry and performance, we're doing the same thing. We're like meaning. So the manifesto offers another context in which we mean what we say in an unequivocal way, and we don't have to question what it is that we heard because we know what we heard. Like I said, it's not implied, it's stated.

DL: I love that because it necessitates a certain new form, maybe. Unless, I guess, that's another conversation—if all manifestos are the same form. Because I have that big book over there of manifesto-isms and they feel like they take the same form in some way too. But they're transparent too.

TM: And that's a choice of the editor, also. I remember when that book came out, I was part of the book party for that book. What I noted was that there weren't women of color represented in that book, except for one person who felt tokenized. Which I said at the party, which was tacky on my part. I also didn't feel well, so I didn't have my filter of "Should I?" But one of the things that I talk about in this book is the cocktail party, and these intimate settings where everyone agrees what everybody believes, just by being there, but suppose you don't? So, even though I think that book is extremely helpful in thinking about a lot of it, it is not an official way of thinking of manifestos, it's a curated way of thinking about a particular type of articulation. So, one of the reasons I mentioned Harryette Mullen and Bob Kaufman is because they're not in that book.

AD: I'm also interested in the relationship between curation and something being official. Like, I think that's so spot-on, you know, in the sense that if a series of objects have been arranged by, you know, an agent, an official person, then my relationship to it is such that I think that it's, that no hand has touched it in fact. You know, the curator sort of disappears and it becomes this objectively great thing.

TM: I should just say before I jump off the mic, that everybody does that, so I'm not, like, mad at Caws for doing that, I'm just noting that since I was invited. (Laughs.) I noted it. But everybody has that subjectivity, so just to be fair.

DL: And you mentioned teaching, and every teacher, as well, makes the same kind of gesture, the subjective gesture that is taken as objective most of the time, or authority…Okay! Second question, for everyone, (laughs) thank you for being excited for my lame questions. What is the imagination? This is something I always want to know. Is it contextless? That's the thing that I always want to know; is it free of context? And is it different for poets than for everyone else? Are we special in the way that it manifests or whatever? Or, yeah. I guess I'll leave it at that.

RSR: I mean yes and no. Sure, we're special in that we're doing poetry and not what someone else might do. For example like the dozens, las decenas or las décimas, which are akin to the dozens in Puerto Rico, or something that was performed in a town in Añasco where my grandparents are from, and las décimas are extremely rhymed competitive verses that have a very concrete structure, and so most of the people who performed them didn't have to know how to read or write, but they were, it was just like a pastime, right? But maybe some people weren't into that, they were into doing something else, I don't know, like my uncle is a carpenter, he's amazing, that's what he does. I mean, I can't do that, right? So, is it different? Are poets' imaginations different? Yeah, in that we kind of are obsessed with this one thing. And someone else might be obsessed with another thing. And then maybe on a smaller scale, just the way we are in the world is an imaginative exercise often, against the very structures that constantly try and restrain that. Even something like seeing figures in clouds is an imaginative exercise. I don't know, I feel like it is contextual in every case, but if we're going to talk about a human imaginary capacity, I do think there is a capacity to be imaginative that humans have. But that's kind of a broad entry point. (Laughs.)

AD: (Turns to DL) Can I answer your question with a question?

DL: Yeah, yes. Oh, with a question? Ok.

AD: Should I go? Ok, because I sort of think the imagination is, like, completely tied to context. And so, then I was like, maybe I'm thinking of context differently than Dottie's thinking.

DL: Well, I'll just say I think so too. I think it's completely tied to context. (Laughs.) But I asked the question just to see what you all thought. (Laughs.) Sorry, that was quite a sneaky manipulative question. Yeah, no, I do think it's completely tied to context. But I want to believe in a contextless place that all contexts end up in, i.e. like an afterworld, which I don't totally believe in. Anyway, that's why I'm asking you all, in the hopes that it'll change my mind, or solidify my opinions. Anyway, I'll shut up. (Laughs.) But, what do you think? (Turns to AD) Oh, okay, the question was the response.

TM: One of the things I wanted to just add…I mean, I think everyone is fundamentally capable of imagination and poetics. I think poetry is foundational to beings, and it's not just necessarily related to humans, you know, it's being. But one of the things I wanted to just emphasize, I had to come to the realization, is that there's a submission. And I submit to this muse situation, I guess that's what you're after. And I'd like to think that I come up with all these notions and ideas, but I don't, I submit to her. It's unequivocal. And, you know, I wish that I could take credit for a lot of stuff, but it's her (gestures to the air above her head), it's her, it's this other thing, and I'm being whispered to and castigated or whatever. It's something outside of the ego, because the ego wants me to, I want to look, you know, I want to be liked sometimes, and I want to sort of put my best foot forward but, but she's got other things that are more important and I have to submit to that, because if it becomes about the ego, then the muse stops. She says, "Oh you're not listening to me? Then go about your merry way." And then you have stuff like writer's block, or choking on your words or something like that, so to the extent that there's a poetic imagination, I defer it to this other entity and I know it's super old-schooled to bring up the muse, but I really do not feel like it's not me, and it's not not me, it's her. So, maybe that's the context.

DL: I agree. Anyway, yeah so now might be a great time for people to ask questions if they want to, we could use this side, we didn't use this side a lot but, does anyone want to ask anything at all? (Laughs.)

AD: It's gonna be okay, nothing to be scared of. (Laughs.)

Q: I just want to thank you all, that was really wonderful. I felt like a common thread in the three presentations was this conversation about… Well, starting with Anaïs, you spoke about this third space, the space of liberation, which is not in which marginalized people are either free or unfree, it's this other carved out space, which you called the deepening of mundanities, which I thought was beautiful. But also, Raquel, when you were talking about the closing of the department at Mayagüez, and how Puerto Rico has to rely on, Puerto Rican poets and writers have to rely on, the weight of poetry, how you can make it look not like poetry and like something essential, I was thinking also of that space. And then, Professor Morris what I loved about your presentation was the creation of the phrases "I mean" and "yeah, but" which you called a search for the middle, which I also thought, it is a great privilege to be able to rest on that structure and know it's going to be there. I wanted to hear you all talk a little bit more about that space.

TM: One of the things I think that…Thank you for your kind comments and close listening…is going old-school. I believe in the nouveau but I also believe in going old-school and not conceding it generationally or any other kind of way. I feel like, in terms of Black Power, that it's something to be wrestled with, and something to be wrested from. You know? I talked a bit about that in more detail, like how do we, you know, we're so used to stuff being appropriated that we say, "Imma make the new thing, I'm gonna make the new thing," but then we sometimes concede the old things that people who will use it as device to make us doubt ourselves, or to destroy ourselves, and I think that's true of all marginalized people. And so I don't think the muse is necessarily about Greek affect, that's just one term for it, or whatever, but you know, it's not like I'm a Luddite, even though, kinda? You know, I kind of need to get off social media, but it's like this…every generation thinks that what they're doing is completely new. And there's a strength in that but there's also a vulnerability in that in that everything else that is a part of their legacy is appropriated and used to disempower them sometimes, I think. So, trying to find the mean, the golden mean, which is a very old-school phrase, or talking about the muses, or talking about Austin, or talking about Bruce Lee (laughs), which I talk about in this book…or even using the term Black Power. It's to reclaim it, to reshape, and one of the things that I got from my colleagues, actually all these colleagues so far, is this fearlessness in terms of negotiating the antiquated with the avant-garde, and not feeling like you have to choose, or that there's only…that there's a binary, because it isn't.

RSR: Well, I think that maybe it's just having been an organizer for so many years in Puerto Rico and having to sit down and explain things as we were taught in my ex-organization, en arroz y habichuelas, you know, in rice and beans, but I feel like, I really want to start in a place, from a common ground, with whoever I'm talking to. And then, I want to do the most I can to really be annoying as shit, like edge them towards a kind of brink. And so in that sense, the middle is just the place where two people meet and my advocating for excess is actually starting there and then just (laughs), kind of, like, really pushing it somewhere else until it's almost unrecognizable. But, I mean, you can come from a place of complete refusal and that has a great deal of value, but at this point in my life, I'm trying to harness all this Taurian energy, so I'm trying to be like, really chill and talk to people more, like, close (laughs) so that's where I am.

AD: My brain went like eighteen million places…but I guess that, what's happening most immediately for me, is thinking about boundaries. And you know, the way in which sometimes we talk about knocking down boundaries as a positive, you know, where, you know, breaking down walls…and it can be a positive, but also sometimes the disintegration of boundaries is a negative, and there are situations where without boundary-ness, the possibility for actual contact broken. Contact as opposed to like, merging, for example. And so I really respond to what Raquel is saying about…(turns to RSR) wait, did you talk about, you talked about contact right? Yeah. Maybe this third space or this mundane space is a space where we're both sort of separate but touching, you know? (Gestures with hands side by side.) It's like, this is you, this is me. And perhaps that that's happening all the time, you know, but that it just doesn't feel that way or seem that way. I think about like… no, never mind I'm not going to go there. But I think about, you know, living in a place like New York where you see so many people each day, right, I'm seeing your faces and in a way I feel deeply connected with you and also I may never see you again. And so is there a way for that to be… meaningful in a lasting way? I don't know, just riffing.

TM (Flipping through Mary Ann Caws's *Manifesto: A Century of Isms*): I'm just looking to see if Kaufman was actually in this book. I know Harryette was not in this book, and that there's just one woman of color in this whole big ol' book. I'm trying to see was…(turns to DL) do you think? Was Bob Kaufman in this book? Just looking. I didn't think so, but I wanted to correct the record if that were the case. A lot of great people in here, I just feel like, you know, like I said, in fairness everybody has their point of view that's important. I think the answer is Suzanne Césaire is the only Black woman in this book. Senghor's in here. But, I guess what, you know, because I'm a poet person, to name a book with just this title, it sounds, seems more encompassing. So, I was like, well if it's not encompassing, it is perspectival and everything is…so, I don't think I see him in here. And, I think, I'm trying to develop the discipline to not necessarily be mad all the time but to be proactive, and one of the things I wanted to affirm was what I love in this, in my first effort here, it's just full of mistakes and it couldn't be in a [inaudible] for sure, to learn what it is and to…it's a declaration of love, too. I think most manifestos are, and I think Wayne, was it Wayne? Maybe it was Ken? We were talking about this idea of love, and universal love and care. And I just wonder how, (turns to AD, RSR) it seems like what you all were saying, and what everybody is saying is not…is asserting this idea of not at the expense of, not at the expense of, you know we assert something but not at the expense of a third-wave medium, whatever. So, I just… it's making manifest and not manifesto as the noun but also the verb of making something manifest that we love.

DL: I was just thinking, I love your triptychs that you set up with the heart being the manifesto. I wrote it down; I don't have it memorized. But, yeah, I love how you kept making three things and they were all setting up to work against each other.

TM: Well I kept failing at writing this damn one post-freaking-dissertation book everybody says you have to write after you finish your dissertation. (Laughs. Looks into audience.) No, you didn't say anything! You didn't get on me. But he was encouraging! And I was just like I can't do it! I wrote three poetry books, but I couldn't get to it. And I said why? And it's like, oh, I was trying to put too much in it. So it was, you know, school of hard knock's constant failure, and we should not be afraid of failure, by the way. Austin talks a lot about failure helping, to embrace that, instead of being perfect and this pressure to overcompensate when you're marginalized and to be perfect because you're judged so much more harshly.

DL: And why can't the poetry book be the dissertation? Why does it have to be a certain form? But I'm just talking…

TM: Oh yeah, well that's another, that's a whole other…well I guess a creative PhD is…but they separate those.

Q (Muffled): Do you write for an audience?

TM: Excuse me?

Q (Muffled): Do you write for an audience?

TM: Do I what?

Q (More clearly): Write for an audience.

TM: Do I write for an audience…

DL: Yeah! (Covers mouth with hand.)

(Audience laughs.)

DL: All of us!

TM: Mmm…no…implied in your question is several things. I feel your passion to respond to a lot of things that you're working through, and I feel like a good direct discourse. But you've asked a couple of questions off the mic. Which implies a privilege of space, you know? That makes this a two-person conversation. Because I can hear you, but it's not for the record. So, I appreciate that passion but it's an interesting sort of choice. I don't write for audience because it implies…a certain sort of relationship to the ego that I've had to release. I write what I feel like I have to write, whether there's an audience for it or not. And I have very good experimental poets that I bow to in that way, like Nate Mackey, like Bob Kaufman, like Harryette, like Fred…you present, you offer, but

I don't know if it's to, it's offering, and an offering, if you think about it, is a gesture, (sweeps hand above the table) is like this. Whereas as (points into the audience) is like this. And it may fail, but I have to do it anyway. There's something knocking on my head that tells me to do this thing. And it's whether or not I want to. So, it's not for an audience, it's in supplication.

RSR: So, I promised myself I wasn't going to get too hyped, But I'm gonna try, I'm going to try…(waves hands in a circular motion while nodding head with eyes closed) I'm trying to do the middle ground thing, like that Aristotelian Golden Mean, that shit that, you know, went straight into Catholicism, was just like a hammer over my head most of life…the middle ground, right? So I'm trying that, without associating it with my grandmother (laughs) and just like this sense of "don't be gay" or whatever, or like, "be gay but not too gay," or whatever the fuck. So I want to come back to this idea of what we're allowed to express and how loudly, or how extensively, and the essay, this, like, five paragraph essay. Because in Latin America, that is not, people don't do that, right? Our best essayists don't write five paragraph essays. They write beautiful, long elaborate essays that are way better than anything that can be taught in a composition course, and they would kill it here. So this idea of following this composition shit that gets taught in like first grade English all the way up until you graduate, that sort of American thing, really to me is like the way that white Americans cook chicken with just a little salt and pepper, like they don't know how to cook! Y'all need flavor in your life! And I don't mean like, shit you appropriate, I mean, like, you don't have it! (laughs) It's not built into you and so, like, to break down form, like form as an abstraction, or the essay as something you got taught in your school in the US as a white American and go back and think about how provincial that is in relation to the rest of the world that's been writing essays since before you were born, like that's the kind of shit where I'm like, really? You're gonna come here and you're gonna talk about that? Of all the things that the US has given the world, which, many of them are bad, the one thing you're gonna fixate on is this thing? That's where I, like, don't get it (laughs) you know what I mean? That's where I can't really vibe it. I don't know, anyway, sorry. I got hyped anyways.

Q: Hi, thank you all. I feel very activated in this thing. I don't usually ask questions that's not really my way. So this is gonna be kind of clumsy. But, I just was thinking, I guess you know, Dr. Morris you were talking about the manifesting, and then Anaïs with your project, I feel like there's this kind of like, I don't know, like metaphysical interdimensional quality to the manifesto that I feel like is implied in what everyone's talking about, but nobody's necessarily saying it. And I don't know if that's just academia and you're not allowed to say that or what, but I'm just curious if you guys could speak just a little bit to the magic? You know, if you feel like you might be doing some magic with these kinds of forms?

RSR: Um…yeah?

(Audience laughs.)

RSR: I don't know. (Laughs.) Yes.

AD: Mmm…I mean, like, manifesting things, or, you know, creation, feels sort of like a kind of magic. So, I think about, yeah I don't know, I guess it's an interesting thing to sort of try to speak directly to the magic, because it's sort of this like…almost the ground we're all standing on, you know? This magic, and then this is what happens from that place. I don't know if that is making sense but it's almost like the magic is what brings us here and what allows us to speak to each other in this way.

TM: Well, it's a great question, it's a very loaded, obviously, question. You know, the etymology is always fun to sort of nerd out on, right? Spelling, right? So before Gutenberg and all of that sort of universalizing literacy, it was magic, right? To utter something, to be incantatory is the heart of poetics. And the economy of poetics, the reverberation of poetics works very well in metaphysics, which is why so much of metaphysical writing is poetic because it's got something extra and the intention, the power of words, not just literally, but in their utterance, the sounds of the utterances and all of that. Because I'm approaching this notion of omni text, of a sonic omni text, as a sound poet and in other ways. I think that's there. I'm not…I don't have a problem with that conversation, the thing that I try to consider, though, is how that leaves out people who don't engage in texts that way. Humanists, atheists, and agnostics for example, who are doing something that is quite metaphysically profound in terms of their relationship to humanness and beingness that's not associated with a higher power, or what they consider any kind of power, but still has that resonance. Like, wow, I'm on Earth, this is what I will do to support. So that's the only reason why I'm cautious, but yeah, I think the origins of poetics and of language comes from people saying, "what hath God wrought" in a way, trying to figure it out and say it in order to be part of it. But it's a great question, and I'm glad you framed it the way you did, about people being afraid of saying it because academia doesn't allow for that. But if we sort of say, instead of what you believe, what's the heart of where this comes from, then people can sort of be in it and be analytical or passionate about it in that way.

DL: We probably have time for one more question.

Q: Hello, thanks so much to all of you. In a way, this is sort of following on things that have already been opened up, but I guess I'm wondering about the essay as a social genre. Anaïs, I was thinking about how you framed your presentation as the essay as conversation, and, Dr. Morris, so much of your essay felt also like a conversation with yourself, like sort of dramatizing the ways we socialize with ourselves. And Raquel, it was from a context of organizing, too, that you're having these reflections and I thought about the fact that, I know at least Raquel, I think for everybody here, everybody was solicited, you know, solicited to write an essay. And sometimes we get solicited to write poems, but more often we get solicited to write essays. There's an economy of essay writing. And I was wondering how you think of the social dimension of the essay and how it's different for you, or if it's different for you, from the social dimension of the poem…or the essay as a social space.

RSR: For me, the essay was the only way I could deal with theory or come close to academia because I just hate so much of the way in which academic writing is framed. The essay was like the only thing that I could kind of be a poet in and still engage with theory in a way that felt nonviolent to myself.

AD: Sorry, I'm just still thinking about the sociality. Like if it's…there's like the tiny sociality of like, I can conjure up other people in my mind, people are passing through my mind as I'm writing, then there's, like, this (points upwards and makes a small circular motion). I think that…I, you know, before reading the thing I read, I practiced it. Which I never practice reading a poem. And so I'm sort of thinking still about what it means to rehearse an essay but not a poem. And there's something about, even in this context, I think I had some anxiety about an urgency behind needing to communicate clearly. And even as I was like, "What does that mean? You don't need to do that," or, "How are these other ways that you can think about it?" There's still, I think, for me, attached to the essay, a very strong desire to pass a message. Where with a poem, I think my desires around what the poem will do are totally different.

TM: I think it's fraught because the origins of my writing come from being in isolation as a sick person, as a young sick person. So I'm comfortable with my own thoughts and keeping my own company. But there's also a responsibility that one has once one becomes a teacher and once one puts one's work out in the world for people to matter and not matter. It's just framing that in a way in which approval, it's not about approval, but what one offers out of love to hopefully make the world one wants to see, is…fraught and it's complex.

DL: Well, I hate to end this conversation, but the good news is we still have more to go. But right now we're going to take a break if you want to take some time to go to the exhibition, or hang around here, or go outside, just save your ticket.

Myung Mi Kim, Cecilia Vicuna

DL: It's really hard to ask questions after that…(Laughs.) But I'll just ask one question and then we can open it up. So, a question I thought to ask you keeping with the theme, is when you look over a wide expanse like a sea, or an ocean, or a field, with snow, what do you think of?

CV: I was thinking of that lantern, because, one of the parts that I didn't read you, is that, some of the things that you sent in the invitation, I had to look up in the dictionary. And while I was looking into the dictionary, I decided to look up the word "snow" and the word "ocean". And ocean comes from the Greek "Okeanos." Of course, a male god. You see the Greek that has come to us is male, is the male conquest of the ancient Aegean Mediterranean culture. And the word snow is Germanic. So, I am reading snow, a Germanic unattested origin, and this beautiful description of the crystals and I'm thinking, "My god, if we carry on the way we are going now, very soon people will only be able to read about snow (whispers) in a dictionary definition." The ultimate colonizing tool. And while I was watching Kim struggling with the lantern, I realized that the lantern was like a crystalline structure, and I thought maybe that's how we're going to relate to crystals: through plastic.

MMK: Yeah, one can begin only when…you just start where you are at. So, if you ask me later, I might say something different, and forgive me in advance because the first thing that sort of starts to…move around in my head, is how these open spaces have actually been poached, and appropriated. So, there's that layer. Meanwhile, that sense of expanse is something that, I think, can allow you to actually have a response to those acts of colonization, and what I like to think of as kind of like the gridding of the world…And, yeah, I mean in some sense the collision of those ways of responding to your question, right, it's been gridded, encroached, devastated, but also as a way of returning to a different reading of those things that are.

DL: I'll ask another one, but maybe people are really wanting to…

CV: You answer first. (Laughs.)

MMK: Okay…(laughs.) I'll try.

DL: I don't know if this is an answerable question…But what is more an agent or material or performance: a poem or an essay?…Or just say whatever you want. (Laughs.)

MMK: You know, I'm going to answer that question probably indirectly by saying that part of what I was trying to maybe…make an opening for, in terms of what I presented today, was to, in some sense, come up with a different way of understanding the circuitry around what we call essay or what we call poem, and to try to invite everyone in the audience, to think about what sort of recements those categories for you, and why? Some of the sort of, disciplinary lines, or what I was gesturing towards as categorical thinking, that to some degree we're subjugated to, consciously or unconsciously. At the same time, I understand that this is how we speak to each other. I mean that, syntax, and grammar, allow us to have a kind of reciprocity and porousness. But, here I'm mostly I guess curious about not trying to nominate one or the other as more or less of something…You know, more agency, less performativity. But to really, in some sense, compound that question, away from their twoness, or…but to see, to a large degree everyone sitting here in some sense, has their own negotiation with how to, in some sense, follow through on designations that are useful. And to what degree thinking and making anything, looks like a kind of unclassifiable, uncodifiable experience of language, intonation, pitches, rhythms, durations, that can't necessarily be capsized in any particular way. And that's when you actually have, I think, an experience of making something or paying attention.

CV: Yeah, I agree with what you say, but also, I could say since you had the word performance in your question, for me...Everything is performance, and everything can be performed. I mean, if you look at the way kids, especially very young kids, relate to language, they're already playing with words, even before they can make full sentences. So, this notion that everything is out there for playing, for pushing, and attracting, and you know moving and so forth, is already ingrained in us. So, what we're doing in a way is recovering the full potential of that, and everything can be performed. (Turns to MMK.) Even at some point of your text, you were performing things that you have, you know, transcribed from some kind of government or propaganda kind of thing, and it was perfectly within the performance. It didn't change at all the fluidity of the movement, because she had set forth this pace already. So, what is really crucial is the where from, is what's said for example...(Turns to DL.) One of the parts I didn't read was that you...one thing that was attractive about your invitation, was that you were calling for a rebellion against the thesis, against the necessity to always do a thesis. And so, I thought, "My God, I was never a part of academia, so I never endured that form of oppression" but if you write it, it must be because thousands of people must be enduring that form of oppression. So, again, I looked up in the dictionary. And how was "thesis" different from "hypothesis"? And the difference is that hypothesis includes the root "hypo" and that root means under, means below, means beneath. So, whatever you are doing in that hypothesis, is yet to be verified. So, it has that mobility of something that does not need to be proven with an argument, or it does not have to be solidified. It has that room for waviness and wobbliness, and all of that. And Mallarmé has a line I probably will misquote, but something like "everything happens as a hypothesis." And everybody, meaning bacteria, living things in the ocean, everybody is hypothesizing, you know? How I'm going to eat you, or how I'm going to survive, or find food. You see, it's this sense of hypothesis, it's a universal thing. So, it's the idea of the thesis that becomes the oppressing thing. But not because the proposition, not because proposing, it's only because you are forced to demonstrate, that is what makes it hard and edgy and really impossible to sustain by how we know reality works.

DL: Yeah, I agree completely with everything that's been said. (Laughs.) Not that that's important, but does anyone want to ask a question and come to our very welcoming microphones? Does anyone want to do that?

Q: Hello, Dottie you read that wonderful poem by Harryette Mullen called "Elliptical" which was such an incredible way of framing, I felt, these performances. And that poem for me has always been so much about, what is left out, what is elided, but also what certain structures of language do to certain communities, and the ways in which they're pointed to, but also erased. And so, I was wondering if these wonderful writers and performers could talk about what the role of the unsaid, maybe what I'm trying to think of is the role of the "under-said", the thing that's not being said but that's being implied. And also, the way that silence and lacunae play a role in your process and in your work?

CV: You go?

MMK (Laughs): I went first last time! (Laughs.) No no, it's fine. I think one way to start answering Emily's question is to, not simply make space for the unsaid, but building more like a duration for that absence, before something can be reabsorbed into that space. So, that the question of silence or lacunae is not so much about marking what is here to...up to that point been occluded, but really in some sense, especially I think in poetry, I think earlier Tracie Morris was using the word "reverberation". So, I do believe silences and lacunae, or elision, I'm trying to think of some of your other words, what is left out, isn't actually a...it's more porous than I think it's trying to include or making gestures for inclusion, but really in some sense rhythmically, intonationally almost, not using, to have an experience.

CV: For me, the unsaid is really the starting point; where are you? In other words, the way I see words and language itself, is completely based on something that is impelling, propelling the need to speak and to say. Which is an impossibility. So, everything that we do is again like a trying, like an essaying. And so, for me, what makes poetry poetry, is that the poem comes from that place, from the awareness of that. From the feeling, the sensation, the being of that. I have said, for example, that what speaks to me, is what is not word inside the words. And this comes from an experience I had as a child. You know? That I saw inside words. And so, that experience continues to be alive in me. So, at the same time, there's something very beautiful about what you just said. (Turns to MMK.) About the duration. And, language has a lot to do with time. Language is a timed operation. You know? Because of sound, it appears to begin and end; of course, it's only a perception. But, in truth, it is a time thing, like they say cinema is a time art, you know, or performance is a time art. And yet, when you have certain experiences, those experiences remain with you forever. So, it is timed and not timed at the same time. It is like quarks; it is local and non-local at once. You see? That is what makes words not codifiable. And I don't think AI will ever get that. (Laughs.)

Q: Firstly, thank you, both of y'all so much, for your essays, those were incredible, so was Brandon's who isn't here obviously. But, Cecilia…this is for both of you, but since you brought up the sort of Anthropocene, I was kind of wondering…that era is a time of necrosis, it's a time of death, but it's also a time of specific types of life appearing, and if there are ways that either of your work reckons with that sort of complexity? I guess to rephrase or reformulate that, I'm kind of thinking of the double meaning that the colony has in it. There's the colony that's of the colonizer, of oppression, of mass death. And then there's the colony that's of insects of wasp colonies, of all these types of life that aren't human, but are also still reproducing themselves in the wake of this ongoing climatological doom. Is there a way that you sort of engage with that life and that death? How does that inform your practice? Does it?

CV: Ok, can you say again the part about the life and death, because I missed the birth.

Q: Just that in the Anthropocene there's all this extinction that's happening, there's this rise of technology, rise of machines, which are causing lots of death, but there's also lots of…as that death is producing rot, there's an increase in types of fungal growth, there's an increase in some insect life.

CV: Inside life?

Q: Insect. Insect.

CV: Oh, okay, (laughs) sorry, my hearing is not so good. So, you're asking if I got it, that the Anthropocene is causing death and it's also causing life?

Q: In some ways, yes.

CV: Yes, I see. Yes, I suppose that is, sort of, one of the things that cannot be avoided. You know? That life and death are really one. I actually have a poem that I did actually in homage to Nicanor Parra, the poet that just died in Chile. He was my friend. And, I knew him when I was a young girl, and I actually visited him just maybe a year before he died. And in this poem, I asked the question, why do we have two words, one called life and the other one called death? Because one is so inextricably mixed in with the other, one makes the other one possible. So, in reality, in Spanish, we have a word for that union and it's called muertevida; life-death, you know? So, what can I say about the Anthropocene? I think, unless we collectively decide that we don't want to go under, I mean disappear, we have to be completely aware of what the machine is doing. You know? Because having created a machine to rule us, which is what we have done, is not in the awareness of a lot of people. And, how else to understand what's going on? You, see? And so, this notion…(Turns to MMK) and it was very present in your fantastic piece, the one about how did you call it? The atrophy. When you were speaking of atrophy, you know? It's like an atrophy of awareness, an atrophy of participation. An atrophy of really thinking of what is going on, and what is our duty to ourselves, and to life itself in this moment. And, as long as we continue to pretend that this is not something to do with our daily acts, really, I don't think the Anthropocene will have much of a chance (laughs) to last very long. Sorry. (Laughs.)

MMK: That is a great question, and the way I'm going to answer it is probably not very directly. But I've been thinking a lot about viability, or, the cusp between viability and non-viability. In all forms of life—machines, ideas. So, I am actually very interested in where the scene of a certain kind of deterioration, or you know, even complete collapse, does perhaps signal, right, as you suggest, new forms of life. And I'm very very interested in that cusp. Again, whether it's an idea, the way that we organize ourselves communally. So, yes. Very much that sense of collapse as a kind of rejiggering, and here I'm very also…given our symposium today, thinking about how new forms of thinking arise, persistently. So, not direct, but. (Laughs.)

CV: Very much to that point I would say, there's one word that is the site of hope. Which is, emergence, what is unaccounted for. What is usually overlooked. Or, ripped out because it cannot be calculated. And this is really what is embedded in every cosmic process including our life here on this planet, you know? And so, it's really the most surprising and eerily beautiful thing.

MMK (Whispers): We're scaring the room.

CV (Pointing): You wanted to speak too?

Q: Hello. My question is, how would one write a poet's essay on geometry, or science, and how can you convey the beauty of poetry, and tangle it with the rigidness of geometry and step-by-step logic, and have those two things work together, or is that even possible?

165

MMK (Laughs): Well, you know, I think back to the etymological root of "essay". I think, all you have in that instance is the effort to try, and seeing what emerges from that, you know…So, what I would like to say, I mean just in general about what we've been talking about today, is… Let's say you wanted to do such a thing, such an essay, but not having any predication or projection about what that might look like, is I think what we've been talking about today, right? In some sense, to be able to unshed yourself from both, a kind of leaning towards something that pre-exists, or anxiety about not be able to meet the conventions of things that you think you should, ought to maybe, comply to. So, part of the challenge and the beauty of the problem as you put it is, can you attempt to do that without having any notion of what that might look like? And would that actually be the essay? Not any worry about it, not any compliance you would have to perform. But the action, or the activity, of finding out.

CV: Yeah, that's a beautiful summation, I think. It's absolutely fantastic. And, before coming here, I was thinking I mean, what do I really want to say about this essay is that I am an essay, you know? And each one of us is an essay. So, if we can connect with that essaying part, in us, then all kinds of things can begin to happen, not only in our writing, but in what matters just as much, or even more, is our behavior. So, for example, in my work, I have always done both; writing and writing with act. Acting in the land itself, by the ocean, with the ocean, in the snow, with the snow; it's something that I have been doing for fifty years. It's something that has been utterly invisible throughout my life. As invisible as can be. And then now, all of a sudden, it's becoming visible. Why is it becoming visible now? Because something is happening in the minds of people in this moment; like this catastrophe that we are enduring. It's really opening people up, all over the world. So truly, there is a chance to encounter in your language, within language itself. That's what I think my poems are dreaming of.

Q: Hello, I also want to say thank you so much for this lovely discussion. I guess a lot of what, and I'm not going to say this is a conflict, but a lot of what we're talking about is about language as a technology. So, implying that it has some kind of utility, and definitely in all three readings today, that was a felt experience, for me at least. But then, saying that a technology can be a kind of an attempt at the same time. And I was just wondering in terms of the utility of the essay, it would be interesting to hear you talk a little bit about that.

MMK: I might need a little help figuring out the question, you want to say a little bit more?

Q: I guess to put it more simply, I feel like a lot of what we're circling today is about the essay, in any form, in a new form and in the entire history of form, from where it came there is a kind of utility implicit in the way we're talking about it. And, I just would love to hear a bit more about your individual or collective understandings about that utility. I was mentioning language as a technology, which maybe was just a take away from your two readings especially. But yes, the utility of it.

MMK: This may not be at all satisfying. (Laughs.) It's just like, yeah… I'm trying to understand the question in terms of, (turns to CV) I think something that Cecilia and I may be aligned a little bit, is trying to notice, and I'll just say this as quickly as I can…I'm just going to circle back to something I said at the beginning of the Q&A, which is that of course the kind of function, or what you're calling a technology, of both, whether it's a form like the essay form, or language as a practice, as a concept, and as a cultural process…I think the tipping point for me, is where the utility actually becomes the only measure for what that utility does. So, for example, if language in some sense is merely replicating its instrumentality—communication to communicate—how's that different from, perhaps whether it's in the work of essay writing or poetry writing—any kind of writing, where you actually try to understand how that technology is acting on you. What is it, how is it seeping into your consciousness in ways that you do and do not anticipate? Or can and cannot tell? And that's I guess where I would try to say, is where the attempt part comes in. Because it's a way of almost exposing and re-exposing the ways in which these technologies become subsumed. Or even, indoctrinated; they're a process of indoctrination. And so, I think it's partly when I say effort, or try, or test, or experiment, or attempt, it's really a sort of perennially questioning, to put in the interrogative, what is this technology? How is it allowing me access to my own field of perception? How is it in some sense performing a kind of occlusion, whether I know it or not? And it's the attempt to catch that.

CV: Wow. (Laughs.) Performing and occlusion. That's exactly what the way language is being used and taught is doing. (Turns to MMK) You, in your text, you use this phrase "the oppression of intelligibility." Think of for example…I will know think of Shimoda, of his beautiful piece. If you are an Indian like I am an Indian, and you have awareness that there is another way of sense, another way of naming, another way of being, you are constantly, or at least I was from a very early age, aware that there was another way. And, how did I get another way? Because my mother—even though she had lost her language three generations before I was born because her people were massacred—she still did not give up, and she's still alive, and she still lives in that other mode, even though she's using Spanish. So, she turns around Spanish, she bends Spanish, to manifest these other dimensions. And that's what was transmitted to me. Now, for example, I have been reading about something called epigenetics, have you been reading about that? It's the most fucking fascinating thing. Because you see, that Western science has been projecting the idea that there's something called "The Selfish Gene" and that genes rule and genetic information rules, nu-uh, it ain't that way. There's something called the epigenetic phenomena, which means that you on the one hand, receive from your ancestors' the genetic information, certainly you do, but you also receive another form of information, that is even more powerful and has the ability to change and alter the genetic information, and this is the epigenetic phenomena. And what causes it, is the likes and dislikes. What you really feel, what you really want to do and what you really don't want to do. I mean, I read that, and I thought this is completely freeing. Because this performing occlusion is preventing us from having access to that infinite freedom that we have inherited. So, when I speak of the machine, what I am really asking, is for us to recover the full humanness of our humanness, you know? Which is something that we are renouncing little by little by becoming extensions of the machine, you see, constantly. So how this is reducing reducing reducing our ability to sense all the dimensions of possibilities for us as a culture, for civilization, for life on earth, you know? So, all the parts I left out, were the parts about the infinite delight. I think, against the oppression of utility and usefulness, our main thing is that (whispers) we're here for and because of this infinite love and light that has moved people for maybe three millions of years.

DL: I feel like that's a good place to end, yeah? (Laughs.) Thank you.

Happiness

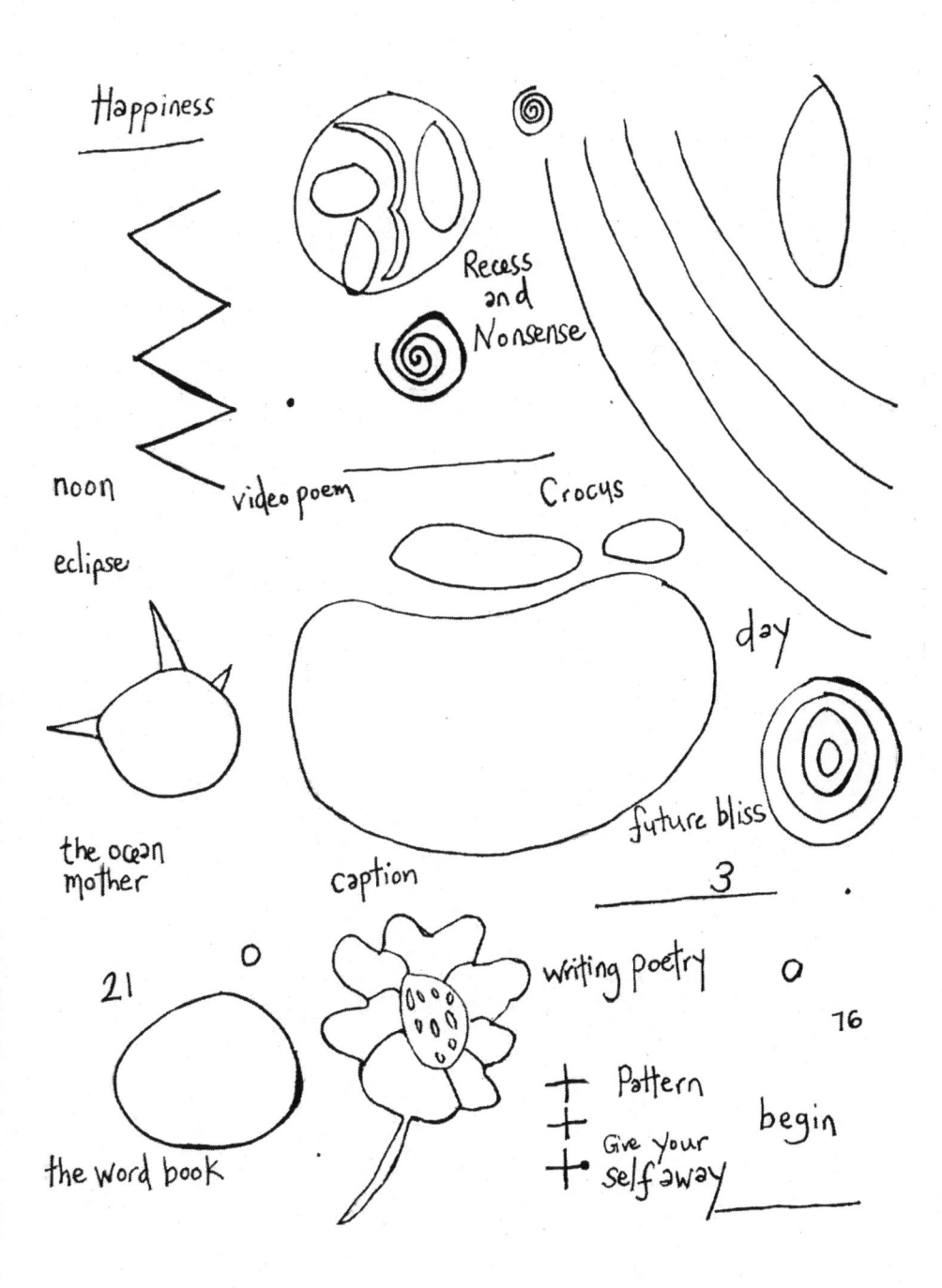

Recess and Nonsense

noon   video poem   Crocus

eclipse

day

the ocean mother   caption   future bliss   3

21   writing poetry

the word book   Pattern   begin
Give yourself away

NOTES

NOTES

ACKNOWLEDGMENTS

So many thanks to Essay Press, who put their belief in this book and gave it a perfect home. Thank you especially to Travis Sharp and Blair Johnson for their endless support and brilliance.

Thank you to Semiotext(e), which originally published Wayne Koestenbaum's "The Cheerful Scapegoat" in his book *The Cheerful Scapegoat: Fables* in 2021.

Thank you to *The Song Cave* and to City Lights who originally published parts of Brandon Shimoda's "Four short and unfinished essays (with poems) from the ruins of Japanese American incarceration" in *The Desert* (2018) and *The Grave on the Wall* (2019), respectively.

Thank you to E.R. Pulgar and Flora Field for their amazing assistance during the making of this book.

The *More than a Manifesto: The Poet's Essay* symposium, held at Columbia University in March 2018, was funded through the generosity of a Lenfest Junior Faculty Development grant, a Dean's grant through the School of the Arts, and funding through the MFA in Creative Writing program. Thank you to all of the wonderful people who made this support possible.

A special, enormous thank you to Carol Becker, Dean of Columbia University School of the Arts, and Gavin Browning, Director of Public Programs and Engagement at Columbia University School of the Arts. Without their visionary support and immense care, the *More than a Manifesto: The Poet's Essay* symposium and this book would have simply not been possible.

A final immense thank you to all of the poets who have contributed to this volume and the symposium—for your work, your spirit, and your radiance.